INSIDE STORIES

INSIDE STORIES

20 Years of Media and Communications at the University of Sydney

Edited by Agata Mrva-Montoya, Cheryl O'Byrne and Pam Walker

The University of Sydney

First published by the University of Sydney

© Individual contributors 2024
© The University of Sydney 2024

Reproduction and communication for other purposes
Except as permitted under Australia's *Copyright Act 1968*, no part of this edition may be reproduced, stored in a retrieval system, or communicated in any form or by any means without prior written permission. All requests for reproduction or communication should be made to Sydney University Press at the address below:

Sydney University Press
Gadigal Country
Fisher Library F03
University of Sydney NSW 2006
Australia
sup.info@sydney.edu.au
sydneyuniversitypress.com.au

A catalogue record for this book is available from the National Library of Australia.

ISBN 978-1-74210-507-9 paperback
ISBN 978-1-74210-508-6 epub
ISBN 978-1-74210-509-3 pdf

Cover image: Maria Barbagallo

Cover design: Diana Chamma and Isabelle Laureta

We acknowledge the traditional owners of the lands on which the University of Sydney is located, the Gadigal people of the Eora Nation, and we pay our respects to the knowledge embedded forever within the Aboriginal Custodianship of Country.

For Anne Dunn (1950–2012)

Contents

List of figures	xi
Foreword 　Catharine Lumby	xv
Introduction 　Agata Mrva-Montoya, Cheryl O'Byrne and Pam 　Walker	xix
1　The birth: beginnings of Media and 　Communications at the University of Sydney 　*Marco Stojanovik*	1
2　Infant program leaps to prominence: MECO from 　2006 to 2013 　*Johanna Ellersdorfer*	15
3　Navigating growth and change: MECO from 2014 　to 2022 　*Pam Walker, Nikbanoo Ardalan and Yonglin (Tina) 　Zhu*	31

4	Convergent media: when MECO met Digital Cultures *Olga Boichak and Chris Chesher*	45
5	In search of a place to call home: MECO buildings *Chris Gillies*	57
6	"The glue that holds MECO together": Digital Media Unit *Alexandra Spence*	67
7	Imparting wisdom: journalists teaching journalism *Tim Piccione*	77
8	Teaching undergraduate students to question, to innovate ... and to push back *Cheryl O'Byrne and Cindy Cameronne*	91
9	Story-making in a global context: the Master of Media Practice *Cheryl O'Byrne and Anna Jenica Bacud*	101
10	"I came because I could find no other degree like it": Digital Cultures *Cheryl O'Byrne*	113
11	Between theory and practice: teaching public relations *Cheryl O'Byrne and Sylvie Chen*	125
12	"A community of practice and professional discourse": the Master of Publishing *Agata Mrva-Montoya*	135
13	Crossing disciplines to improve lives: the Master of Health Communication *Olaf Werder*	151

Contents

14 Building confidence and courage: internships 161
   Kiran Gupta

15 From *The Korea Herald* to the *Bangkok Post*: 173
   Overseas Fellowship Program
   Weien Su and Cheryl O'Byrne

16 "A critical part of the MECO family": higher degree 183
   research students
   Agata Mrva-Montoya and Penny O'Donnell

17 Enlarging perspectives: networks of domestic 195
   research partnerships
   Jenny Welsh

18 Going global: the internationalisation of MECO 207
   Pam Walker

19 How to survive a pandemic 221
   Rebecca Bowman and Victoria Wills

20 Digital and post-digital futures for communications: 235
   MECO in the 2020s and beyond
   Terry Flew

MECO timeline 245

About the authors 249

Index 261

List of figures

Figure 1.1 Catharine Lumby with Charlie aged four months, 2000   3

Figure 1.2 Anne Dunn, mid to late 1980s   8

Figure 2.1 Catharine Lumby at MECO 10 year party, October 2010   17

Figure 2.2 Anne Dunn at MECO 10 year party, October 2010   19

Figure 2.3 Fiona Giles in her role as Postgraduate Coordinator hosting a PG "Welcome to Media and Communications" event at Sydney University Village, July 2006   21

Figure 2.4 Steven Maras on Faculty of Arts delegation visit to Centre for Advanced Study in Social Sciences at Fudan University, Shanghai, October 2010   22

Figure 2.5 Megan Le Masurier, Fiona Giles and Louise Katz at Student Union, July 2006   23

Figure 2.6 Gerard Goggin, Anne Dunn and Fiona Giles, August 2007   24

Figure 2.7 Fiona Giles, Anne Dunn and Steven Maras hosting a delegation of visiting media scholars from Denmark, May 2006   26

Inside stories

Figure 2.8 Anne Dunn at MECO 10 year party, October 2010	27
Figure 2.9 Jonathon Hutchinson, 2022	29
Figure 3.1 Joyce Nip with Alana Mann at SLAM Christmas party in 2016	32
Figure 3.2 Justine Humphry, Alana Mann and Steven Maras at the ANZCA Conference in July 2017	35
Figure 3.3 Gerard Goggin at SLAM Christmas party in 2017	41
Figure 3.4 Fiona Giles and Benedetta Brevini with Steven Maras at his farewell party in March 2015	42
Figure 4.1 Chris Chesher	47
Figure 4.2 Terry Flew, 2022	54
Figure 5.1 RC Mills Building, 2024	59
Figure 5.2 Transient Building	60
Figure 5.3 Holme Building, 2024	61
Figure 5.4 John Woolley Building Level 2 entrance, 2022	62
Figure 6.1 A broadcast exercise in Semester 2, 2023	70
Figure 6.2 Phil Glen and Shelagh Stanton filming and recording at the ANZCA conference in 2017	72
Figure 6.3 A broadcast exercise in Semester 2, 2023	74
Figure 7.1 Bunty Avieson and Pam Walker with the students participating in the first MECO Newsroom, 2019	78
Figure 7.2 Bunty Avieson, 2022	80
Figure 7.3 Lea Redfern, 2019	81
Figure 7.4 Fiona Martin, 2012	86

List of figures

Figure 7.5 Penny O'Donnell, 2022 — 87

Figure 7.6 Margaret Van Heekeren, 2022 — 88

Figure 9.1 Intense focus as students polish their filming skills at an April 2016 presser — 102

Figure 9.2 Student prepares for a presser in May 2015 — 104

Figure 9.3 Students filming during a MECO presser in April 2016 — 107

Figure 9.4 Students filming during a MECO presser in April 2016 — 110

Figure 10.1 Marcus Carter, 2023 — 115

Figure 10.2 Justine Humphry, 2017 — 118

Figure 10.3 Olga Boichak, 2023 — 119

Figure 10.4 Mark Johnson, 2021 — 120

Figure 11.1 Mitchell Hobbs, 2023 — 126

Figure 12.1 Agata Mrva-Montoya, 2016 — 139

Figure 12.2 Cover of *Earth cries* (2021) — 146

Figure 13.1 Olaf Werder, 2018 — 152

Figure 14.1 Adriana Hernandez, 2022 — 166

Figure 14.2 Lauren Castino, 2024 — 170

Figure 15.1 Overseas Fellowship Program fellow Hamish Boland-Rudder in *The Korea Herald* office, 2011 — 174

Figure 15.2 Richard Broinowski at his farewell party in 2014 — 178

Figure 16.1 Benedetta Brevini, 2022 — 187

Figure 17.1 Diana Chester, 2024 — 198

Figure 18.1 Richard Broinowski, Robin Moffat, Steven Maras and long time Australian Embassy liaison Jinny Lee at YTN 24 hour news channel. Seoul, South Korea, 2010. 209

Figure 18.2 Tim Dwyer, 2016 212

Foreword

Catharine Lumby

In 1999, as a freshly minted PhD graduate and practising journalist, I was given the extraordinary privilege – call it luck if you like – of designing the University of Sydney's first media and communications degree. MECO degrees were previously seen as "trade" degrees suitable for teaching only at non Group of Eight universities. But their popularity saw them increasingly integrated into sandstone universities where there was a general wariness about teaching subjects that did not "belong" in the traditional humanities.

Most degrees in the media and communications field at the time were badged as journalism degrees. And journalism had only recently been seen as something worthy of studying at a tertiary level. Journalists, the professional wisdom dictated, learned everything they needed to know in newsrooms, not in ivory towers. I clearly remember being hired at *The Sydney Morning Herald* fresh out of doing an Arts/Law degree at the University of Sydney and proudly showing the editor my CV. He put it in the bin and told me: "That's irrelevant. I'm hiring you because you can write."

It was an era where research-intensive universities were suspicious of offering media and communications degrees, while mainstream media industries were suspicious of their value. The University of Sydney's MECO degree helped quell those doubts. One of the most important principles that has always grounded teaching in MECO is equipping students with the skills to enter and navigate the volatile media and communications industry sector, and to think critically while doing so.

An excellent humanities education, grounded in a degree that allows students to major in traditional humanities subjects, equips them with the ability to think critically, to research and to communicate clearly and persuasively. It also challenges them to think about the role of journalism and what we now call media content production in our democracy and our society.

Many of our graduates have gone on to have stellar careers in journalism and increasingly in strategic public relations, political communication, public policy and research, and publishing. Today, many of them will also build careers in areas like social media strategy, galleries, libraries, arts and museums, as well as game design and mobile media industries.

A wonderful addition to the MECO discipline was the merger with Digital Cultures, led by Chris Chesher and Kathy Cleland. As media and communications practice and research became increasingly focused on the digital, the complementary program offered by Digital Cultures brought critical analysis of the role of the internet in transforming the media landscape to bear on teaching professional skills and provided students with subjects that helped them navigate the changing media landscape. The merger was also transformative for MECO

Foreword

colleagues in their own research. A longstanding collaboration ensued.

The university sector has also evolved over the past two decades and has increasingly welcomed international students. There is no doubt that local students have benefited from this, as have their international classmates. For my MECO colleagues, integrating the experience and needs of international students was an opportunity to strengthen our focus on the global impact of our teaching and research. In a more concrete sense, teaching a large group of international students alongside local students is a fantastic opportunity to get them talking about how media and communications operate in diverse cultures and political systems.

From the early days, MECO has also been a leader in giving students from a wide variety of backgrounds and cultures access to education. Early on, we implemented an alternative entry pathway for students who did not have high tertiary entrance scores. The University of Sydney has traditionally been associated with students from privileged backgrounds, but in MECO we have always been passionate about social justice and inclusion in our teaching and research. When it comes to journalists and media content producers, it is very clear that diversity is still sorely lacking in Australia, and we are committed to being part of the solution by providing educational pathways for everyone.

The astonishing thing for me, looking back over the history of MECO, is the extraordinary number of brilliant researchers who have worked in the degrees and equally been passionate teachers. I can't do the roll call, but this book tells the story. We have also produced amazing graduates, many of whom my colleagues and I are still in touch with and actively mentor.

Inside stories

Reading this book, I have been struck by the extraordinary journey of colleagues and students over the first two decades of the history of the Department of Media and Communications. A department that started as a small undergraduate program with high ambitions has grown into one of the most respected media and communications programs in the country, with five postgraduate programs. MECO PhD graduates have gone on to influence the field internationally.

For me, the most wonderful endorsement of the hard work and passionate engagement of my colleagues is when a journalist calls me to set up an interview and says: "You won't remember me, but I was a MECO student, and the incredible lecturers inspired me to become a journalist. Now, can you talk about your research?"

All of us at MECO remain passionate about both teaching and researching in ways that make a genuine contribution to society and to solving very pressing, big picture problems. Join us. We are good at conversations because we are experts in communication.

Introduction

Agata Mrva-Montoya, Cheryl O'Byrne and Pam Walker

It has been over 20 years since the Media and Communications (MECO) program was established at the University of Sydney. It has been many years more, though, since the University first embarked on the teaching of journalism, as we discovered thanks to Penny O'Donnell while writing this introduction. Among the books in her office, O'Donnell has a copy of *Wayward sojourn: Pioneer tertiary journalism education in Australia*, a master's thesis by Glen Coleman, completed at the University of Technology Sydney in 1992. Four journalism diploma courses began in the 1920s: at the University of Western Australia, the University of Melbourne, the University of Queensland, and the University of Sydney, the latter of which ran from 1926 to 1931.

As Coleman writes: "In Sydney, the course almost immediately fell apart through apathetic non-attendance; appalling failure rates; mutual antipathy between journalism and academe, and newspaper rivalry (both particularly severe in genteel Sydney); and, finally, absence of funding." The course awarded only one diploma in 1930, to Kenneth Hutton

Wilkinson. The University of Queensland hosted the only journalism diploma course that thrived in this period. It took until the 1950s for other Australian universities to establish and sustain journalism courses and until 2000 for the University of Sydney to do the same.

In February 2020, the MECO staff met at a two-day retreat to discuss plans for the year, including ideas for 20th anniversary celebrations. At some point during the retreat, the idea for a book arose. It was envisioned as a collaboration between staff and students, modelled on the University of Sydney Anthology project, and aiming to capture stories about teaching and research at MECO in 20 chapters.

Then the COVID-19 pandemic hit. The University campus closed down in March 2020 and plans for a celebratory party were shelved. But we kept working on the book through the pandemic, regularly meeting on Zoom. And we continued working on it for many months afterwards. The project took far longer to bring to the finish line than any of us had expected. Students joined, and then moved on. Colleagues struggled to find the time to contribute. Competing priorities and unrelenting workload pressures kept getting in the way. In the end, it took over three years to write and review the chapters.

While we did fill some of the gaps in the discipline's institutional knowledge, this is not a history book. *Inside stories* contains a mix of reportage-style pieces and essays written by students and academics in 2020–22 about the research, teaching, people and infrastructure of MECO. They reflect the opinions and experiences of those who were available to talk to the contributors. Not all were, for various reasons, and the uneven coverage remains a key weakness in

Introduction

the journalistic pieces. Despite these shortcomings, the book contains fascinating insights, perspectives and moments chronicled to preserve the rich tapestry of our discipline at the University.

This book shows the dynamic landscape of media and communications in the first two decades of the 21st century and demonstrates how a discipline can keep reinventing itself in this context. The first three chapters look at the history of MECO. Chapter 4 focuses on the merger with Digital Cultures. Over the years, MECO staff members have occupied offices across several buildings at the University, and Chapter 5 chronicles these movements. Chapter 6 looks at the role of the Digital Media Unit in supporting the discipline's research and teaching. The following chapters (Chapters 7–13) provide insights into the teaching across undergraduate and postgraduate degrees, focusing on the pedagogy of theory and practice and how these have evolved over the years. The chapters on internships (Chapter 14) and overseas fellowships (Chapter 15) showcase successful programs that have been a distinct feature of MECO education. The following three chapters focus on research at MECO: the higher degree research program (Chapter 16), and national and international research collaborations (Chapters 17–18). The book then turns to look at MECO during the COVID-19 pandemic (Chapter 19) and concludes with the future of the discipline (Chapter 20).

An edited collection about the history of a department sounds like a vanity project, but in the process of working on the book we learned much about the importance of collective knowledge and accumulated wisdom that shapes institutional culture, guides decision-making and informs future directions.

Inside stories

In a world characterised by rapid change, institutional memory serves as a bridge connecting the past to the present, allowing an organisation to draw upon past successes and failures to navigate current challenges. By providing a sense of continuity, institutional memory provides context and helps preserve core values and identities while fostering growth and adaptation. It is not simply a catalogue of what has been – it is a crucial tool that informs what could and should be.

This has been a long journey, and we would like to thank all the students and staff who contributed to the book, agreed to numerous interviews, and responded to endless emails with requests for extra information and clarification. We are particularly grateful to Catharine Lumby, Penny O'Donnell, Margaret Van Heekeren, Gerard Goggin, Steven Maras, Fiona Martin and Rod Tiffen. Steven Maras has been invaluable in making the book more accurate and thorough.

Special thanks to the many students who volunteered to research and write chapters while working on their assessments (many also holding down a job): Nikbanoo Ardalan, Anna Jenica Bacud, Rebecca Bowman, Cindy Cameronne, Longtong (Sylvie) Chen, Johanna Ellersdorfer, Chris Gillies, Kiran Gupta, Tim Piccione, Marco Stojanovik, Weien Su, Jenny Welsh, Victoria Wills and Yonglin (Tina) Zhu. We would also like to thank Emily Garnett for her contribution.

We are grateful to Elizabeth Connor, Bethany Cannan, Marcus Miller and Robert Crompton for their help with collating data and facilitating access to various files. Many thanks to Maria Barbagallo for the photos and Diana Chamma for designing the cover.

Finally, we would not have been able to complete the project without the help of Sophie Belotti who copyedited the manuscript with care and attention to detail, Holly Ford who

Introduction

meticulously proofread the first pages, and Chelsea Sutherland who created the index. Chelsea Sutherland and Isabelle Laureta took care of typesetting and finalising the design of the book. Thank you so much.

The ensuing chapters invite you to delve into our past, witness our struggles and successes, and anticipate our future. This book is more than just a historical account – it is a collection of inside stories about our department's unyielding spirit and a tribute to the enduring power of a dedicated group of people.

1
The birth: beginnings of Media and Communications at the University of Sydney

Marco Stojanovik

Three weeks after giving birth to her first child, Catharine Lumby was preparing herself for another kind of birth. It was October 1999. In February, the first ever Media and Communications degree at the University of Sydney – a Bachelor of Arts (Media and Communications), a different degree than the Bachelor of Arts, with its own Universities Admission Index (UAI) requirements – was due to enter the world, and she, as its director, was responsible for its design. Some nine months earlier, Bettina Cass, the Dean of the Faculty of Arts, had appointed her to the role. Lumby had just four months to finalise the structure and write full curriculums for two first-year units before 100 students would be entering the lecture halls.

Her partner brought their baby to her office each day to be fed. Sitting with her baby became Lumby's daily highlight, a brief respite from a busy schedule planning to implement her vision of media and communications education. Having completed her PhD in media studies at Macquarie University the year before and working in journalism for 13 years prior, she had a good idea of what she wanted to achieve.

Throughout both her academic and journalistic work Lumby had always been deeply interested in human rights and experiences that were not captured by the mainstream media, particularly around the issues of gender, sexuality, and race. She strongly believed the fourth estate could shed light on such issues, expose abuses of power and inform the public about their rights. For her, the media practitioner's role was a vital one: to enhance democracy by writing or broadcasting information in a way that served the public interest.

To achieve this, she knew students required more than production-based skills: they also needed a broad knowledge of the world and the ability to interpret information critically. Therefore, in addition to production subjects and an internship, the degree would include core theoretical subjects including Media Studies; Media Relations; and Media, Law and Ethics. Students would also undertake a second major in Arts or Economics. The 2002 degree brochure describes the program in terms of both "a vocational perspective" and "an academic perspective": "the degree is focused on producing students with a portfolio of practical skills who also have the general knowledge and critical intelligence which comes from an excellent humanities education".

The University of Sydney, a prestigious 150-year-old institution renowned for research within its Arts faculty, was an ideal place to provide this sort of education. To understand why the University established a media and communications degree – and why it took so long – it is instructive to begin in 1964. This is when the Menzies government put in place a binary system of higher education. On one side was the academic and research-oriented university sector – the older

1 The birth

Figure 1.1 Catharine Lumby with Charlie aged four months, 2000, photo by Duncan Fine

established universities supplemented with newly created ones – and on the other side was a new advanced education sector, which grew out of former teachers' colleges and some technical and agricultural colleges.

Some teaching of media and communications in Australian universities dates back to at least the 1950s, but the 1964 expansion of higher education marked a "major impetus for growth in degree level studies."[1] Media and communications studies developed within the vocationally oriented advanced education sector, and similar courses were then developed at the newly established universities.

Within two decades, communication studies courses were established in at least a dozen tertiary institutions around Australia.[2] The emergent discipline was enriched by the

---

1   Putnis et al., 2002, p. 5.

establishment of the Australian Communication Association in 1979, along with two affiliated journals. Henry Mayer, professor of political theory at the University of Sydney, founded *Media Information Australia* in 1976 (renamed *Media International Australia* in 1995) and, in the same year, Rod Miller founded *Australian SCAN: Journal of Human Communication* (renamed *Australian Journal of Communication* in 1982).[3]

Still, the older universities "showed little interest" in a communications degree.[4] This began to shift, however, following another set of restructures to higher education. In 1987, the Hawke government introduced the "Unified National System", which ended the binary system and merged 85 tertiary institutions into 37 large-scale universities. A raft of vocational courses that had been developed within the advanced education sector were brought into the university sector. This included media and communications courses, which were incorporated into restructured Arts faculties.[5]

At the same time, the government took action to increase student numbers and create a more egalitarian higher education system. Adapting to a diversified student body and a new emphasis on vocational relevance required a greater range of curriculum offerings. This was happening against the backdrop of the revolution in communications technologies that accelerated through the 1990s and created a demand in the labour market in Australia and its neighbours.[6]

---

2   Putnis, 1986, p. 143.
3   Wilson, 2006; Petelin, 2013.
4   Irwin, 1998, p. 275.
5   Putnis et al., 2002, pp. 6–7.
6   Putnis et al., 2002, pp. 6–7.

1 The birth

Research in the field was continuing apace. In 1990, communication was included as a formal field of research category in the Australian Research Standards Classification.[7] In 1994, the Australian Communication Association was expanded and reconstituted as the Australian and New Zealand Communication Association.[8]

From 1989 to 1999, Australia saw a three-fold increase in student load in media and communications courses. By 1999, media and communications courses were offered at 27 institutions and, according to a May 1999 Department of Education, Training and Youth Affairs census, communication studies had the highest student load of any discipline in the humanities group at Australian institutions.[9]

Many of the older universities, feeling market pressure and the need to remain relevant in the new university environment, began to offer media and communications courses. Faculty minutes from 3 November 1997 contain a report from a working party led by Stephen Garton exploring whether the University of Sydney should join the trend.[10] The report identified a number of pre-existing units across Education, English, Government, Law, Sociology, Women's Studies and the Sydney College of the Arts that could be incorporated into such a program. Moreover, there was some existing production equipment across Arts, Education and the Sydney College of the Arts. The working party concluded that there was "sufficient staffing, curricula and equipment resources within the college to begin a substantial initiative in the field of media

---

7   Maras, 2006, p. 44.
8   Wilson, 2006, p. 17.
9   Putnis et al., 2002, pp. 22–25.
10 Faculty of Arts, 1997.

and communications", but with a need for more investment in the future to ensure the reputation and attractiveness of the program. They also pointed out that the success of such a program would "depend on the establishment of sound institutional and industry links".

The benefits of the proposed program were clear. The working party found, "On intellectual grounds the analysis of media and communications has become a central field of inquiry in the humanities and social sciences. The number of staff already offering units and conducting their own research in these fields is testimony to its significance." Moreover, the University of Sydney was the only university in the region without a media and communications degree, even though the degree was becoming a significant criterion in student university selection and attracted high calibre students. The faculty approved the recommendations to establish a program of study in media and communications and appoint a director for five years, tasked with coordinating existing resources, planning a structured program of curriculum development and working with a planning group, which included Barbara McDonald (Law), Neil Becherwaise (Education), Rod Tiffen (Government), and Su Baker (Sydney College of the Arts). This is how Lumby, appointed as that director, came to be at the University.

When Lumby stared out across her lecture theatres that first year, she saw 100 brilliant young people who had worked diligently to achieve the high UAI required for admittance to Sydney's newest degree. In MECO1001/1002: Introduction to Media Studies 1 and 2, she taught them the key concepts, methodologies, theories, and interdisciplinary roots of the field.

Production units followed in the second year. Students learned the theory and practice of radio and online broadcast news, the basics of writing news and features for print and online media, and practical skills required for media relations and advertising industries.

Lumby taught these production units in 2001, with assistance from Geraint Evans, deputy director and lecturer at the Language Centre, for MECO2001: Broadcast News (Radio and Online). Soon she was given the opportunity to recruit more lecturers and expand the range of production-based units.

Her first recruit was the late Anne Dunn, who had graduated from the University of Sydney with an honours degree in Education in 1972. Dunn had extensive experience working as a presenter and researcher for television and radio in Australia and the UK, as well as lecturing at Charles Sturt University in Bathurst and Western Sydney University.

"Anne Dunn was the most wonderful colleague to work with," Lumby told me. "An expert, supportive and ethical, she was absolutely critical in the development of the degree and the department. Her legacy is written into every aspect of teaching and research we did and still do."

In her video production unit (MECO3001) Dunn introduced students to the history, theory and practice of video production, both field- and studio-based. She helped equip students with skills in planning, researching and budgeting a video production, as well as in digital camera operation, video recording and video editing.

But Dunn's particular love was radio. She felt it was the most effective way to communicate as it allowed a direct connection between her and her audience without interference from other people in the production or communication chain.

Figure 1.2 Anne Dunn, mid to late 1980s, photo taken by an ABC staff photographer when Anne was a radio presenter, courtesy of Anne's family

Students in her radio broadcasting unit researched, scripted, recorded and edited a radio news magazine item. The course also looked at the history and contemporary status of radio and considered the role of the internet in audio broadcasts.

However, these production units were a slow starter for Dunn as the University lacked adequate media production infrastructure such as studios and specialised computer labs – an issue common among the universities that were new entrants to the communications field. This was in stark contrast to the specialist facilities offered by the newer universities at which Dunn had previously worked.

1 The birth

Media and Communications was succeeding, but it still struggled to establish legitimacy at the university. Many looked upon it as merely a vocational discipline, somewhat inferior to the established Social Science, Arts and Humanities disciplines the faculty had built itself around.

Lumby encountered this attitude frequently in the early years.

"Oh, you're a journalist, are you? People like you don't do research, do you?" Lumby remembered being asked by an English professor.

Lumby laughed as she recounted the interaction. She said she was used to people thinking journalists were "anti-intellectual" and "untrustworthy". The media and communications degree would prove them wrong, as students developed strong research skills in an intellectually demanding environment.

By the time Lumby was setting up the degree, most undergraduate media courses at Australian universities combined research with practice.[11] There had long been tension, though, over the orientation of the research component.

Helen Wilson's 2001 Australia and New Zealand Communication Association's presidential address describes the "cross-current" of traditions that influenced the early years of the field in Australia. One current was the American approach, which had a strong emphasis on applied psychology and media technique and tied the field to commercial activities including advertising and public relations. The other current was the British approach, which had a Marxist orientation

---

11   Putnis et al., 2002, p. 38.

toward critique and tied the field to cultural studies, structuralism, linguistics and semiotics.[12]

Peter Putnis's 1986 review of communication studies in Australia pointed to "the growing influence of Anglo-European perspectives at the expense of earlier American-inspired approaches".[13] The confluence of the two paradigms, and predominance of the cultural studies approach, was evident in the University of Sydney's curriculum.

In 2003, Lumby hired Kate Crawford. While also completing her PhD, which resulted in the book *Adult themes: Rewriting the rules of adulthood* (2007), Crawford created an online media production unit. The unit examined the development and growth of the internet and provided a critical framework through which to understand the way it was changing the media landscape. The unit also had a practical component, with students gaining skills in writing and producing for the web and learning to design and develop their own websites.

Crawford went on to become a widely published researcher, academic and author examining the politics, impacts and social implications of large-scale data systems, machine learning, and artificial intelligence. Although it was unusual for someone to be hired as a lecturer before completing their PhD, Lumby saw her potential. From very early on, she recognised the value of the insights Crawford provided about digital media as an emerging key component of media and communications.

Many of Crawford's former students are now working in the digital media industry, and one is a professor of digital

---

12 Wilson, 2006; Putnis, 1986.
13 Putnis, 1986, p. 154.

media herself. "Some students thought they would never have to engage with the digital side of things, but now it's a given," Crawford told me.

Lumby further built the degree by recruiting Marc Brennan in 2004. Having completed a PhD in creative industries/media at the Queensland University of Technology the year before, Brennan brought a specialisation in the theories of cultural studies and media studies, and their relation to contemporary industries.

Brennan took on two existing units, MECO1001: Introduction to Media Studies and MECO3605: Media Globalisation, transforming them week by week over his first year. He infused the courses with theories such as semiotics, postmodernism, feminism and queer theory.

Brennan was known for his ability to engage students with contemporary topics, exploring media case studies within these conceptual frameworks. For him, theory and practice could not be separated. He intended to equip students to think about the politics of representation before they began to write, record or produce. He saw the urgent need to discuss these topics, particularly how ideologies and concepts of national identity shape ways of thinking and might influence the way a story is presented.

Richard Stanton also joined in 2004. He arrived with a wealth of industry experience, having worked in public relations, journalism, editing and publishing. He took over MECO2003: Media Relations, previously taught by Lumby and then Dunn.

Stanton guided students to critically analyse the historical and contemporary relationships between the media and public relations. They analysed material drawn from stakeholders in the media relations and advertising industries while also learning necessary practical skills, including how to write basic copy, prepare press releases and information kits, and develop a campaign strategy, budget and timeline. Stanton's book *Media relations,* published in 2007, arose from teaching this unit.

Lumby also considered law and ethics to be an important theoretical and practical inclusion in media and communications. From 2002, she and Dunn alternately taught a unit titled MECO3003: Media, Law and Ethics, which introduced third-year students to key legal and ethical issues relevant to journalism and the professional fields of public communication. Students were given an introductory survey of the main ethical theories in Western thought to establish a framework within which to examine specific ethical issues that relate to media. They were also introduced to the structure of Australia's legal system and to those aspects of the law that impinge on the work of media professionals. The 2003 book *Remote control: New media, new ethics* (2003), edited by Lumby and Elspeth Probyn, is a legacy of their work. It includes chapters by a number of University of Sydney scholars and PhD students including Dunn, Kath Albury, Milissa Deitz, Ghassan Hage and Duncan Ivison. Dunn's work on the unit also led to the book *Media, markets and morals* (2011), co-authored with Edward H. Spence, Andrew Alexandra and Aaron Quinn.

Steven Maras was recruited to the University of Sydney in 2005, mainly to teach video production units. He also took over MECO3003: Media, Law and Ethics. Maras had completed his PhD in communication studies at Murdoch University and worked for 10 years as a lecturer at Western

1 The birth

Sydney University. This was his first time teaching ethics, drawing from a philosophical research background evident in his PhD dissertation *The hermeneutics of production: Extensions of the return to Bergson*. He was instructed to interweave the teaching of ethics and law with discussions and debates around media practice.

"This was in line with the dual commitment of the degree to both scholarship and professional practice: an educational not just training commitment," Maras told me. "Catharine wanted the degree to light an intellectual fire in the students."

He used $500 that Lumby gave him to buy several ethics textbooks and recreated the unit. The unit was to focus not just on the laws and ethical considerations a practising journalist needed to know, but also on broader philosophical questions about the nature of government, law, social ethics and public interest. The idea was that if students could understand their role as journalists and carry this out responsibly, they could flourish individually and make a positive contribution to ethical debate in society.

By the time the Media and Communications program formally became a department in 2006, theoretical subjects based around media studies, the implications of digital technologies, cultural studies, and law and ethics complemented practical units on print, video, radio, online production, and media relations. Students were provided a well-rounded education, capped with a compulsory internship and an optional honours year. By the end of the undergraduate degree, students were well equipped to enter the workforce in a wide range of media and communications related industries.

Postgraduate students soon followed, completing the Master of Media Practice on offer from 2004 (see Chapter 9).

All students left with production skills, broad knowledge about the world learned from wider subjects in the Arts faculty, and the ability to analyse and share information critically and ethically.

Lumby's "baby" was truly up and thriving, with the path set for the next 15 years of expansion.

Works cited

Faculty of Arts (1997). Report of Working Party on Developing an Interdisciplinary Program or Program in Cultural Studies, Media and Communications. Faculty Minutes, Sydney University Archives.

Irwin, H. (1998). Communication studies in Australia: Tensions and new challenges. *Communication Education, 47*(3), 274–85. https://doi.org/10.1080/03634529809379131.

Maras, S. (2006). The emergence of communication studies in Australia as "curriculum idea". *Australian Journal of Communication, 33*(2–3), 43–62.

Petelin, R. (2013). The *Australian Journal of Communication* (1976–2013): Tracing the Trajectory. *Review of Communication, 13*(4), 302–315. https://doi.org/10.1080/15358593.2013.867069.

Putnis, P. (1986). Communication studies in Australia: Paradigms and contexts. *Media, Culture & Society, 8*(3), 143–157. https://doi.org/10.1177/016344386008002002.

Putnis, P., Axford, B., Blood, W., & Watson, L. (2002). *Communication and media studies in Australian universities: An investigation into the growth, status, and future of this field of study*. Division of Communication and Education, University of Canberra.

Wilson, H. (2006). Thirty years of MIA: A commemorative editorial. *Media International Australia, 119*(1), 3–20. https://doi.org/10.1177/1329878X0611900102.

2
Infant program leaps to prominence: MECO from 2006 to 2013

Johanna Ellersdorfer

In the short space of six years, MECO had evolved from a program with a single staff member to a dynamic media and communications department. The place of such a program at one of the oldest sandstone universities in the country was initially questioned, particularly by more traditional academics in the Arts faculty. Surely a program with such a strong vocational focus was more at home in one of the newer universities. However, the program's unmitigated success gave the field of media and communications a foothold at the University of Sydney. It was an experiment that had clearly paid off.

The years between 2006 and 2013 was a period of consolidation. It was a time of further cementing and building on the efforts of foundational staff to develop a course that gave a new generation of journalists the tools and theoretical framework necessary to face the rapidly changing media landscape of the early 21st century. As well as having proved its place at the University of Sydney, it differentiated itself from comparable courses at other universities by grounding theoretical and practical media education within the humanities, with half the degree subjects drawn from the Bachelor of Arts program.

One lunchtime in 2021 I spoke to Catharine Lumby over the phone. Our conversation meandered through the early years of the department up to today. She explained the history of the department, piecing memories together into a timeline as we talked. Our focus continually returned to the teaching rationale. She is clearly a passionate educator, with a great deal of respect for her colleagues and pride in the achievements of the department.

Throughout our conversation, the importance of teaching students both technical skills and theory was a recurrent theme. Lumby emphasised that "tech skills were taught to ground storytelling capacity". In designing the program, both she and Anne Dunn had an eye for the ways in which the industry was changing. They predicted the impact the internet would have on the media industry and responded practically to increased job insecurity and the rise of the gig economy, placing importance on flexible and adaptable skills in their teaching approach. Within the course, students were encouraged to build a range of skills across audiovisual and written media with no option to simply specialise in print, media or radio journalism. They were also required to complete a second major within their Bachelor of Arts.

Lumby referred to the approach as an "Ikea model" of teaching, in which different skills could be flat-packed and assembled in response to individual jobs and specific storytelling requirements. With a firm belief that narrative underscored many of the potential pathways students might take, ranging from journalistic work to marketing and advertising, the aim was to teach principles that could be

2 Infant program leaps to prominence

Figure 2.1 Catharine Lumby at MECO 10 year party, October 2010

adapted and translated in different formats, across what would hopefully be a long career. According to Lumby, the philosophy of the department was "not about content, but about helping someone form themselves, and their desire and capacity to learn".

Dunn and Lumby encouraged students to think critically, as well as reflect on who they were and what they wanted. With a cohort capped at 100 – something that was implemented from the commencement of the program – it was possible to take a very personalised approach, and they would speak individually to each student entering the program, asking them, "who are you, what do you want to achieve, and how can we support you?"

From its inception, the degree attracted a high calibre of students. With a Universities Admission Index (UAI) over 99 for local students, it was widely perceived as an alternative to Medicine and Law for high achieving students. This high bar of entry was not intentional, but the result of limited capacity imposed by specialised facilities such as the media labs.

A significant downside of this was that the cohort lacked diversity. Lumby was matter of fact when she told me, "We were very concerned about increasing the number of Indigenous students, which I know was dear to Anne's heart, and also increasing the number of low SES students because a lot of the students we got at undergraduate level had gone to private or selective schools."

Together, Lumby and Dunn identified alternative entry pathways offered by the University, and applied these to their program to allow students to apply for the course based on the submission of an essay, portfolio or work experience. Reflecting on these pathways, Lumby continued, "We do know that actually it's not the young people with high ATAR [Australian Tertiary Admission Rank, replaced UAI in 2009] scores that necessarily succeed. You can have people with much lower ATAR scores who, if they're well and properly supported, can thrive." Moreover, the Master of Media Practice (see Chapter 9) was a conversion degree with no

2 Infant program leaps to prominence

Figure 2.2 Anne Dunn at MECO 10 year party, October 2010

requirement for previous study in media, offering a pathway for students who had not studied media in their undergraduate degree and wanted to change career directions.

In addition to the Master of Media Practice, three more postgraduate coursework programs were introduced: the Master of Strategic Public Relations in 2006 (Chapter 11); the Master of Publishing in 2007 (Chapter 12); and the Master of Health Communication in 2009 (Chapter 13). These courses, according to Lumby, "took off quickly" and further expanded the student body, attracting a combination of mid-career local students and international students, predominantly from mainland China. Regarding the implementation of the postgraduate courses, Lumby said, "The idea was to provide learning and career opportunities for local students looking to go back to university and add to their CVs, and also to provide opportunities for international students, and our view was always that local and international students could learn from each other."

Steven Maras told me that during this period links were forged with Fudan University, especially around the Health Communication degree. Fiona Giles and Dunn also negotiated an annual agreement whereby *China Daily* selected one of its journalism staff members to complete a Master of Media Practice and, in exchange, supported a MECO master's student to complete an internship in Beijing.

Maras described the department in this period as "effectively still in growth mode", noting that the student numbers at postgraduate level were "remarkable". These courses were fee-paying and brought in large amounts of revenue to the University. Hearteningly, in the early years of these postgraduate programs, some of this money was put directly back into the department and used to hire more staff, including Fiona Giles, Alana Mann, Sean Chaidaroon, Penny O'Donnell, Fiona Martin, Tim Dwyer, Antonio Castillo, Megan Le Masurier and Joyce Nip. Gerard Goggin also joined the department in 2006, bringing his Australian Research Council (ARC) Australian Research Fellowship. These staff were at the cutting edge of research into journalism and media practice, new media policy, and convergence.

Despite the expansion of the department in this period, there were also some notable departures. In late 2007, Lumby left to take up a new position at UNSW as establishment director of the Journalism and Media Centre. Kate Crawford joined her, as did Goggin as deputy director. Maras noted that Lumby's departure was "a blow to the discipline", but the faculty was very supportive. Dunn stepped into the role of department chair, a position she held for only a year before,

2 Infant program leaps to prominence

Figure 2.3 Fiona Giles in her role as Postgraduate Coordinator hosting a postgraduate 'Welcome to Media and Communications' event at Sydney University Village, July 2006, photo courtesy of Steven Maras

in recognition of her managerial talents as associate dean and co-chair of the undergraduate committee, she was seconded to the role of pro-dean and then acting dean of the faculty in 2009–10. In 2009, Maras took over the position of department

Inside stories

Figure 2.4 Steven Maras on Faculty of Arts delegation visit to Centre for Advanced Study in Social Sciences at Fudan University, Shanghai, October 2010, photo courtesy of Steven Maras

chair, followed by Marc Brennan in 2011. The demands on the faculty at this stage were huge. As Maras reflected, "we were all senior lecturers and lecturers being asked to do extraordinary things".

Infrastructure and digital media support was still an ongoing issue. Maras remembers working on an extensive needs analysis for the department in 2010 with then head of school Tim Fitzpatrick and Phil Glen as an external consultant. This followed the demise of the Arts Digital unit, which was the blueprint for the emergence of the Digital Media Unit (see Chapter 6). The Arts Digital unit was launched in 2009 to

2 Infant program leaps to prominence

Figure 2.5 Megan Le Masurier, Fiona Giles and Louise Katz at Student Union, July 2006, photo courtesy of Steven Maras

provide a central point of contact for all support in the Faculty of Arts.

During this period, staff also focused on balancing teaching and research alongside involvement with the industry. This seems to have stemmed, in part, from the fact that staff had been industry practitioners prior to moving into academia and now maintained those connections. Lumby told me that "none of us were afraid to go out into the media – many of us had been journalists – and talk about ideas, and actually take our research out there, rather than just sitting in our office and writing another journal article." Staff were encouraged to go on TV, talk to newspapers and write opinion pieces.

Figure 2.6 Gerard Goggin, Anne Dunn and Fiona Giles, August 2007, photo courtesy of Steven Maras

Marc Brennan told me that, in the early years, "students weren't that interested in theory, frameworks, evaluating arguments – critical practice in general". He explained that this attitude changed over time, influenced by the lecturers who modelled the integration of theory and practice in their own work.

In 2010, using funds allocated for a professor in the area, the department celebrated 10 years since its inception by appointing Peter Fray, then publisher and editor of *The Sydney Morning Herald,* as the First Decade Fellow. Maras described this as "an attempt to build bridges between education and industry at a scale not often attempted". Fray used the fellowship as an opportunity to research the changing landscape of journalism, focusing on the role of the editor.

This echoed industry concerns that Lumby and Dunn had also attempted to address in their teaching approach.

In early 2011, Goggin returned as inaugural Professor of Media and Communications, and assumed the role of chair a year later. Also in 2011, Olaf Werder came to MECO and began coordinating the Master of Health Communication.

Despite these additions, Maras noted that 2011–12 were difficult years. There was a significant university restructure, which saw staff members, including Brennan and Antonio Castillo, leave to take up opportunities elsewhere. Then, in 2012, Dunn died from breast cancer. Her loss was felt throughout the department, as well as by many former students whom she had generously mentored. Dunn had been critical to the success of the department. She was, as Fiona Martin recalls, an important bridge between academia and industry, bringing the world's public service media research conference, RIPE, out of Europe and to the Asian region for the first time, and engaging the Australian Broadcasting Corporation (ABC) and Special Broadcasting Service (SBS) as partners in the conference program.

Dunn's managerial and broadcasting expertise had been crucial in helping to build MECO, but perhaps more important was what Lumby remembers as "her ethical, professional, calm sense of judgement, and her kindness". In 2014, a scholarship was established in her name, supported by the Journalism Education and Research Association of Australia (JERAA), Australia and New Zealand Communication Association (ANZCA), and Dunn's mother and siblings. In Dunn's memory, it supports excellence in research in communications and journalism for the public benefit.

In 2020, Penny O'Donnell, a member of the department since 2008, won this award for her contributions to the

Figure 2.7 Fiona Giles, Anne Dunn and Steven Maras hosting a delegation of visiting media scholars from Denmark, an early visit as part of Anne's long term interest in Public Broadcasting in Denmark, May 2006, photo courtesy of Steven Maras

industry and research, particularly her work examining job losses in journalism under the auspices of the New Beats project. In her application, O'Donnell reflected on Dunn's influence on her own career, noting her dedication to collaboration, student-focused journalism education and her "unwavering resolve to foster news media change". In summing up, she wrote: "Anne taught me that work for change required vision, hard work, administrative finesse and persistence, but would only blossom and endure with care, good humour and shared values."

2 Infant program leaps to prominence

Figure 2.8 Anne Dunn at MECO 10 year party, October 2010

Dunn is remembered fondly by many in the department. Alana Mann told me, "I recall most of all her wonderful smile and laugh, and the way she made me feel at home when I transitioned to academia from corporate life." Timothy Dwyer also remembers her as being "very welcoming" when he joined the department in 2008. Both Mann and Dwyer speak of Dunn as a mentor, with Dwyer noting that "she had a great sense of the institutional dynamics at the University" and Mann describing her as "always enthusiastic and a great listener, genuinely interested in people". In 2019, Mann dedicated her book *Voice and participation in global food politics* to Dunn, "whose beautiful voice will always be missed by those of us lucky enough to have known and loved her".

The year 2013 saw MECO and Digital Cultures merge (described in detail in Chapter 4), and the arrival of Benedetta Brevini, Grant Bollmer and Jonathon Hutchinson. Brevini joined MECO in 2013 as lecturer in the political economy of communication. A former journalist in Milan, New York and London, she embarked on an academic career at London's City University and Brunel University, and has been investigating the relations between communications, politics, power and inequality.

Bollmer joined MECO as a lecturer in Digital Cultures. He came to MECO from Massey University and received his PhD from the University of North Carolina at Chapel Hill. Bollmer ran the Technology and Culture Reading Group from 2014–15.

Hutchinson was appointed in May 2013 to teach Online Media, and he immediately set about revitalising MECO's cross-media curriculum. Building on the work of Martin and Crawford, he developed an exciting combination of analytics, community focus, digital communication and visual literacy. Soon after joining MECO, Hutchinson completed his PhD in the field of social media research at the ARC Centre of Excellence for Creative Industries and Innovation at the Queensland University of Technology.

When I asked Lumby about the philosophical approach she and Dunn ascribed to in developing the program, she paused

2 Infant program leaps to prominence

Figure 2.9 Jonathon Hutchinson, 2022, photo by Bill Green

for a moment and then responded with a quote attributed to Yeats: "Education is not the filling of a pail, it is the lighting of a fire." Perhaps this is an apt metaphor for the early, consolidating years too. The program was a place where theory and practice met, providing both students and staff with opportunities to learn and develop as researchers, teachers and industry professionals, with a multitude of potential pathways ahead of them. It challenged the traditional curricula of the University, providing an enriching and nurturing environment where careers began and evolved, often shifting in unexpected ways in response to a world in which journalism was rapidly being redefined.

3
Navigating growth and change: MECO from 2014 to 2022

Pam Walker, Nikbanoo Ardalan and Yonglin (Tina) Zhu

The second MECO decade saw a growing internationalisation of the curriculum, which increasingly emphasised digitalisation, interdisciplinarity and industry collaborations. Above all, there was a huge growth in student numbers, especially postgraduate, and an associated expansion of staff.

Until the beginning of 2012, student numbers and university funding were regulated by government-imposed caps on enrolments. The move to the demand driven system was one factor that influenced the growth in MECO's student numbers. The MECO degree offerings tapped into a demand for greater knowledge and skills in new media technologies. But with climbing student numbers, it was becoming difficult to provide sufficient production spaces, labs, studios and offices for teaching staff. This lack of adequate space was exacerbated in these years.

"It was an exciting time in the department," Alana Mann said. "We were growing really fast and we never had enough room for our staff so we all had to move offices a couple of times."

Figure 3.1 Joyce Nip with Alana Mann at SLAM Christmas party in 2016, photo courtesy of Maria Barbagallo

Responding to this growth in 2014, the department changed location on campus. Moving into the John Woolley Building was an important moment in MECO history. It was also regarded as an achievement: after years of being scattered across campus with difficulties accessing proper spacing and resources, MECO could finally settle down.

It's no surprise, then, that when we interviewed staff who were involved in MECO at this time, they all gave similar responses. In answer to our first question – "What do you think is the biggest challenge MECO has faced from 2014 until now?" – everyone mentioned the increase in student numbers.

"Incredible growth in enrolment, incredible success, almost too much success for us to handle; just overwhelming," Mann said. The number of full-time MECO students grew over 90 percent between 2014 and 2020. During the same period, the overall number of students at the University of Sydney grew by more than 42 percent.

Bunty Avieson recalled: "Because we had so many students, there was a lot of pressure on the teaching." A senior lecturer in journalism and media, Avieson started teaching in 2015 – news writing at postgraduate level and literary journalism and media theory at undergraduate level – while also taking care of the student internship project.

The staff we interviewed mentioned other challenges too, identifying four key factors that brought significant change: internationalisation, digitisation, interdisciplinarity and industry collaboration.

Internationalisation

The internationalisation of MECO took place over time as the department participated in international collaborations and events with academics from other universities. The department also made efforts to attract scholars with international backgrounds to join MECO and more globally oriented subjects were taught as part of the curriculum.

When Fiona Martin arrived in 2008, approximately 5 percent of the undergraduate MECO cohort was made up of international students. By 2023, it was roughly 30 percent. The growth in international student enrolments was even greater in the master's programs. "Seeing the expansion, particularly of the Chinese international student cohort, was amazing," Martin said. "And it certainly really challenged us to think about how we could work better with students from different cultural backgrounds."

Lecturers needed to figure out how to teach a cohort of students who had not come through the Australian high school experience, and so had different cultural expectations of higher education. They had to consider, for example, the impacts of students growing up with the Confucian system, which focuses more on mastery through memorisation, standard tests and the respect for teachers as experts, and places less emphasis on cultivating self-directed learning, independent argument and critical thinking.

Internationalisation of higher education in Australia, and worldwide, has evolved rapidly over the past two decades, driven in part by competition in the higher education sector, global flows of students, and increased international opportunities for academic research collaborations and teaching exchanges. Initially, internationalisation at the University of Sydney took the form of scholarships for international students, study abroad exchanges and the introduction of international studies curricula. More recently, the focus has switched to international research collaborations, strategic partnerships, and more inclusive and diverse learning cultures. In 2018, the Academic Board endorsed "cultural competence" – defined as the ability to engage ethically, respectfully and successfully in intercultural settings – as one of nine specific skills graduates will emerge with at the end of their degree.

Margaret Van Heekeren, who joined MECO as a lecturer in 2017, noted that "The increase in international students has had a positive impact in ensuring that content isn't too Australia-centric. Whilst it is important to have a predominant Australian focus, given the degree is based in Australia, having larger numbers of international students is a great reminder, when preparing content, of inclusivity."

3 Navigating growth and change

Figure 3.2 Justine Humphry, Alana Mann and Steven Maras at the ANZCA Conference in July 2017, photo courtesy of Maria Barbagallo

The MECO department now teaches a modern and globalised curriculum, but Penny O'Donnell remembers when the curriculum looked very different. O'Donnell first came to MECO in 2008 as a senior lecturer in international media and journalism, and has had a significant role in shaping MECO courses for over a decade. She was tasked with teaching theoretical subjects, while expanding them to have an international focus that examined the global media landscape. At the time, there wasn't much comparative media research within a global context and she remembers the field as being "old-fashioned". Comparative media research was largely based on a book published in 1956, *Four theories of the press*, which divided the world into authoritarian, libertarian, social responsibility and Soviet communist media.

There were only 12 units of study on offer for those studying a bachelor's degree in MECO, with only one subject looking at media in an international context – MECO3605: Media Globalisation. "The unit focused on global market forces such as cheap labour in developing countries and environmental issues rather than the complex differences between media landscapes in different countries," O'Donnell said.

O'Donnell realised she also had to adapt the curriculum for postgraduate international students, since they made up the major cohort of enrolments. MECO6926: International Media Practice became a core unit in the postgraduate curriculum and the University now offers several subjects focused on global media landscapes, including USSC6920: US Media: Politics, Culture, Technology; MECO6929: Chinese Media Studies; and ASNS6908: Media Industries in East Asia.

"[International students] don't necessarily come to the University of Sydney to learn about Australian media," she said. "They come to learn about the media and most media these days is understood as global."

In the Master of Media Practice (Chapter 9), the international student cohort is extremely high – up to 90 percent in O'Donnell's experience. She considers the pool of international students a precious resource when teaching in classrooms, especially with her emphasis on media diversity.

"For me as a lecturer in international media and journalism, it's just like heaven because you're teaching international media with international students," O'Donnell said.

3 Navigating growth and change

Digitalisation

Digitalisation of media industries, with the rise of digital media platforms, has been another big trend over the last decade. "That's been challenging for everyone because it has moved so fast," Martin said.

The merger of MECO and Digital Cultures (DC) into a single department in 2013 (see Chapter 4) stimulated research into digital technologies, though a number of MECO academics were working on digital technologies and cultures well before the merger with DC. The merger has also facilitated an expansion in the teaching of new technologies in the MECO program.

Martin noted that podcasts have become an increasingly popular student choice, evidenced by the growth in popularity of MECO6941: Podcasting. The 2022 launch of a podcast research centre, HIP: Hub for Innovation in Podcasting, reflects the direction and needs of MECO's third decade. In addition to Martin, the podcast centre team includes Siobhán McHugh (MECO), Lea Redfern (MECO), Mark Pesce (honorary associate in Digital Cultures), Amanda Tattersall (Sydney Policy Lab and School of Geosciences), and Mim Fox (University of Wollongong). In the same year, Mark Ledbury, director of the Power Institute, pitched a new centre for visual communications, and the podcast team aims to contribute to this centre by focusing on the audio aspect of visual communications.

"When I asked students about five years ago how many wanted to go into journalism, I think we were down to about 12 percent," Martin said. "That was five years ago so it's probably even lower now. We still have students that go into journalism careers [but] I think there is far more interest in things like digital influence work and community management. I think there's a heavier focus on visual media."

While the journalism skills of writing, interviewing, research and analysis are crucial for every media graduate, the dynamic media landscape has called for new media skills. Over the past decade, MECO has introduced units to teach social media, using data to tell stories and working with online platforms.

"What employers need from university graduates has changed. Some of them welcome media students because it doesn't matter what business or company they are, they have to engage with the media. They have to understand how to work with the media because it's just so ubiquitous. Media is so much a part of every day," Martin said.

Interdisciplinarity

Over the past decade, MECO has become more interdisciplinary, not just with digital cultures but also working with colleagues in political science, the China Study Centre and other disciplines. "I've worked with the US Study Centre as well. We've become more and better networked into other faculties. We've done stuff with Law and Medicine for example," Martin said. "There's been a push across the sector to be more interdisciplinary because we know that interdisciplinary research is more effective."

Martin was among the seven writers, including Gerard Goggin, Ariadne Vromen and Kim Weatherall, of *Digital rights in Australia*, a 2017 report.[1] "That was basically myself from

---

1   Read more at https://papers.ssrn.com/sol3/papers.cfm?abstract_id=3090774.

3 Navigating growth and change

a strong media studies background, Gerard from a strong internet and media telcos background, Ariadne from political science and Kim from law. What it enables us to do is use our different lenses to highlight the problems that overlap and how we can solve these, so it's a great problem-solving strategy," she said.

Another benefit of interdisciplinarity, according to Martin, is that MECO has become a stronger research group. "Before we were an autonomous and quite eclectic group of researchers. We had a much stronger focus on written research. I think we are a much more collaborative, more multimodal group of researchers than we were."

"When I first came, we were a young department. We'd only been around for 10 years and were all quite junior, apart from a couple of people. During the last decade we have really ramped up our research capacity. We've won more ARC research grants; we have a much stronger HDR program, more coherent and better run [see Chapter 16]. Thanks to Jonathan [Hutchinson] and Bene [Brevini] for that. Now we'll have three professors and hopefully more into the future. I'd love to see us have a professor of Indigenous media studies."

Avieson shares that view: "Now we have people that are researching climate communications, food security, labour practices of journalists, the internet, global media, intermediation and so on. When we do get the opportunities to share our research with each other, then you find that's fabulous."

In 2017, the Sydney Research Excellence Initiative – SREI 2020 – was created. The new program aimed to help University researchers test new ideas, push disciplinary boundaries and identify ways to scale up their research. Exploring digital rights and governance in Australia and Asia, led by Gerard Goggin, became an important part of the project.

Industry collaboration

Another major change since 2015 has been an increased focus on working with industry and holding more public forums and debates. Martin identifies O'Donnell's *New Beats* project, which examines job loss in journalism around the world, as one important example of this.

"I think that doing industry-linked research has become more important and will do into the future." Martin also cites work her team did with Facebook on mitigating hate speech and the work that Hutchinson and colleagues are doing with Instagram as examples of industry-linked research.

Building on MECO's links to industry at the faculty level, Martin has been leading the Work-Integrated Learning (WIL) Project. WIL is not only about getting students ready for the workplace, but also helping them in starting a business, inventing things, volunteering or undertaking further research. As Martin explained, the idea is to provide students with "more strategic and inclusive opportunities for experiential learning, and to develop more applied professional contexts for students to demonstrate key graduate capacities such as cultural competence, inventiveness and ethical responsibility."

The present

In March 2020, the University of Sydney directed its staff to work from home in response to the COVID-19 pandemic (see Chapter 19). Student enrolment numbers did not drop

3 Navigating growth and change

Figure 3.3 Gerard Goggin at SLAM Christmas party in 2017, photo courtesy of Maria Barbagallo

dramatically as feared but online Zoom classes replaced on-campus engagement. The restrictions imposed due to COVID-19 particularly affected MECO's production-based units teaching hands-on skills. Closed borders for most of 2020 and 2021 temporarily stemmed the flow of international students into Australia, a trend that changed once borders reopened. After two years of online classes, much of the teaching has moved back to campus.

The pandemic also affected research productivity in the department, as academic staff had to cope with increased teaching load, additional caring responsibilities at home during lockdowns and inability to pursue field work and travel.

In 2021, Catharine Lumby returned to MECO and became chair. The same year, MECO also welcomed Terry Flew, who moved to Sydney from the Creative Industries Faculty at Queensland University of Technology, Brisbane.

Inside stories

Figure 3.4 Fiona Giles and Benedetta Brevini with Steven Maras at his farewell party in March 2015, photo courtesy of Maria Barbagallo

The year 2022 brought significant change. Alana Mann left for the University of Tasmania. On 1 August 2022, the Department of Media and Communications became a discipline within the new School of Art, Communication and English. There were 34 continuing academic staff and 216 sessional lecturers teaching across three undergraduate degrees: Bachelor of Arts/Bachelor of Advanced Studies (Digital Cultures), Bachelor of Arts/Bachelor of Advanced Studies (Media and Communications), and Bachelor of Arts and Bachelor of Laws (Major in Media Studies), with 1,657 undergraduate students (across the major and minor programs, advanced coursework and honours). There were 1,181 students across five postgraduate coursework degrees (Master of Media Practice, Master of Strategic Public Relations, Master of Publishing, Master of Health Communication and Master of

3 Navigating growth and change

Digital Communication and Culture). There were 28 students enrolled in higher degree research.

Looking to the future, Martin is urging the University to respond to the needs for digital infrastructure at MECO. "It has been problematic for staff but equally for students to be across certain technologies," she said, adding that "staff are feeling they are lagging in teaching, lagging in capacity to deliver that workplace-ready environment we've addressed in the last two or three years." However, she has welcomed the appointment of more permanent staff as a godsend. In 2022, Agata Mrva-Montoya, Catherine Page Jeffery, Joanne Gray, John Hartley, Margie Borschke and Xiang Reng joined MECO. Gerard Goggin returned from his three-year appointment at the Wee Kim Wee School of Communication and Information at the Nanyang Technological University, Singapore. More staff followed in 2023, with Meizi Su and Ben Egliston joining the team.

In 2023, the postgraduate degrees have been reviewed as part of a Faculty of Arts and Social Science-wide process looking at the strategic purpose, curricular coherence and sustainability of the faculty's overall portfolio of postgraduate coursework offerings. It has also been an exciting year for research, with Terry Flew being awarded an Australian Laureate Fellowship for his project Mediated Trust: Ideas, Interests, Institutions, Futures. Moreover, in September 2023, Olga Boichak and Ben Egliston were awarded two prestigious Australian Research Council Discovery Early Career Researcher Awards.

No doubt, the evolving nature of digital technology and society will continue to shape the discipline for years to come (see Chapter 20). MECO will continue to be an exciting and dynamic area of research and practice.

4
Convergent media: when MECO met Digital Cultures

Olga Boichak and Chris Chesher

The year is 2013. Amazon releases its first promotional video of a delivery drone. Facebook introduces audio calls on Facebook Messenger. Apple launches the iPhone 5S model, equipped with FaceID, the fingerprint recognition system and the smart voice assistant Siri. The Oculus Rift virtual reality headset developer kit is released from a Kickstarter-funded start-up called Oculus. 3D printers enter the mass market. Apple Watch is not yet released, but wearable technology is becoming more popular, with gadgets such as Google Glass, Nike+ Fuelband and Samsung Galaxy Gear available. With manifold increases in computational power, machines have become capable of recognising objects and translating speech in real time. Meanwhile, somewhere in London, a consulting firm – Cambridge Analytica – creates a Facebook personality quiz that would lead to one of the biggest political scandals in recent history.

The year is 2013, and Digital Cultures is an innovative cross-disciplinary program at the University of Sydney, interrogating the social and cultural impacts of new digital media technologies such as those above. It convenes the Digital Cultures undergraduate major, the Master of Digital Communication and Culture (see Chapter 10) and has a research profile in new media arts and sociotechnical change. However, it is a program, not a department, and has only 2.6 staff. At the same time, Media and Communications is a successful department with over 15 staff focused on journalism, media industries and practices in the context of rapid sociotechnical and industry transformation. It convenes a boutique undergraduate degree and four master's coursework programs, and its staff has a diverse research profile in media and communications studies.

The year is 2013, and Digital Cultures and Media and Communications, which had worked in parallel in the same school for over a decade, are poised to merge. Together they will be perfectly positioned to make sense of the deep social and technological transformations the world will experience into the future.

From Arts Informatics to Digital Cultures: 2000–13

The precursor to Digital Cultures, the Bachelor of Arts Informatics, was founded in 2000 through a cross-faculty partnership brokered by Julian Pefanis (Art History and Theory) and Alan Fekete (Information Systems). This was a ground-breaking cross-disciplinary degree that combined a major in Information Systems with an Arts Informatics program stream comprised of ARIN-coded units taught in the School of English, Art History, Film and Media (SEAFAM).

The first unit of study to run was ARIN1000: The History and Theory of Informatics, developed by Annemarie Jonson.

4 Convergent media

Figure 4.1 Chris Chesher, photo courtesy of the University of Sydney

Jonson taught this unit for one year before she went on maternity leave, at which point Kathy Cleland, with a background in new media arts curation, and new media artist John Tonkin joined Arts Informatics. The program developed a deeper focus on new media technologies in the arts in Australia and internationally. David Teh also taught in the program.

Chris Chesher joined as director of Arts Informatics in late 2004, moving from Media and Communications at UNSW, which was among the first degrees to focus exclusively on new media. In this capacity, he designed a Research Methods unit, which surveyed cross-disciplinary research methodologies and enhanced an existing Technocultures unit. With his colleagues he proposed and developed a new postgraduate coursework program: the Master of Digital Communication and Culture, which would first run in 2006.

Arts Informatics was a pioneer in games studies, mobile media studies, internet studies and new media arts, without limiting itself to any one of these nascent fields. Its interdisciplinary roots connected media studies, cultural studies, media arts, science and technology studies, sociology, philosophy of technology, and human–computer interaction. Tonkin developed a unit of study called Computer Games and Simulation. Cleland recalls that there was a strong focus on digital arts and online/virtual communities in the early years of the program, including the world-class Digital Arts unit, which was highly praised by students and is offered by the program to this day. Christine Crowe, who transferred into Arts Informatics from the Department of Sociology and Social Work, developed the unit Cyberworlds.

Arts Informatics was active in Sydney's art and technology scene, co-organising anti-conferences through the *Fibreculture* network in which speakers seeded themed round-table discussions, rather than presenting papers. For Justine Humphry, who first joined the program in 2011, the value of the program was in "occupying the space between the utopian imaginaries and the dystopian critiques of emerging technologies".

Ironically, its level of innovation was probably why Arts Informatics had trouble reaching its ambitious enrolment goals: in a culture polarised between arts and technology, the esoterically named degree did not cut through to enough high school leavers. Today, it is customary for students to take a Digital Cultures Table S major from within a Computer Science degree, and vice versa. Arts students can learn programming or design computing. Back then, however, enrolments in the Bachelor of Arts Informatics were not high enough, and it accepted its last intake in 2007. Beyond this decision, the program re-emerged as the Digital Cultures undergraduate major and the postgraduate program, which both proved to be increasingly popular over the following years.

Fiona Martin recalls that Digital Cultures scholars were "years ahead of their time" in understanding the implications of an increasing uptake of digital technologies across arts, commerce, government, media and entertainment industries, at a time when these industries were slow to adopt and adapt to ubiquitous digitisation. Humphry affirms this view: "Historically, what was happening in Australia in the industries was that the internet, and the communities involved in it … were forging a path and leaving telecommunications and the traditional media behind … Those were two alternative development pathways."

Through the 2000s, it became apparent that the concerns of Digital Cultures and of Media and Communications were converging, with the increasing digitalisation of media industries, the rise of digital media platforms and a crisis in the funding of traditional journalism. A range of new digital media emerged, including Web 2.0, social media, platform entertainment, artificial intelligence, search marketing and the internet of things. Internetworked, mobile, locative and automated hypermedia technologies could not be ignored as they were increasingly impacting upon the territories of legacy media industries.

A merger between Digital Cultures and another department was mooted as early as 2007, but there was a long process of consultation and negotiation. As well as consulting with MECO, there were talks with the Department of Art History and Film Studies as another possible merger partner. While merging with MECO seemed a natural fit, some MECO staff observed that the department already had expertise in digital media. Others asked whether a merger might complicate the department's remit, considering the complexities of managing a Digital Cultures major in addition to the four-year named degree, Bachelor of Arts (Media and Communications). But Martin, an early internet adopter in arts and community media and the first MECO lecturer to teach into the Digital Cultures program, saw this development as mutually beneficial; Digital Cultures would bring much-needed insights into research and teaching in the department, while MECO would have a resource base to expand practical offerings for Digital Cultures students. Digital Cultures staff were in favour of the merger but insistent that they should retain their unique identity and control over their curriculum and research directions.

In October 2011, after extensive consultation around a proposal from Digital Cultures, the recently appointed head of school, Annamarie Jagose, formally proposed the merger to the Dean's Executive Committee. The submission argued that "'Digital cultures' remains vital in new humanities curricula internationally". It identified many benefits for the combined department that would prove prescient: the merger

"Strengthens MECO's coverage of new digital media technologies ... Enables curricular collaboration ... Offers a distinct major as an alternate study option for many students ... Sharpens the profile of the Master of Digital Communication and Culture ... [and] Facilitates research collaboration". The proposal offered a detailed course of action for merging the activities and cultures of the two areas over 2012.

In January 2014, the fully merged department moved from their separate spaces in the Holme Building and Level 3 in the John Woolley Building into the freshly refurbished offices on Level 2 of the John Woolley Building, making the partnership material.

In hindsight, MECO and Digital Cultures staff recognise this merger as a true partnership, rather than MECO acquiring Digital Cultures. Per the official press release announcing the merger of two programs, "the amalgamation of the Digital Cultures Program with MECO will enhance both areas, and the burgeoning field of digital cultures research".

Cleland remembers the merger "was a forced marriage. Both parties were initially reluctant, but the Digital Cultures team saw the writing on the wall, and we did our best to make the most of the situation. Luckily, after the merger, we found that we actually did really like each other quite a lot. Over time MECO and Digital Cultures have grown closer, and have definitely benefited from each other's course offerings and collaboration, so now it's become more of a love match."

In the immediate aftermath of the convergence, many MECO units incorporated the digital transformation, as evident in their changing titles: Media Globalisation became Digital Media Globalisation, and Media and Communications Landscapes received a digital prefix before its transformation into Work 4.0. Digital Cultures units also changed focus, with the Web Production unit changing to Web Transformations and then Internet Transformations. Cyberworlds became ARIN2620: Everyday Digital Media.

Then, in 2016, the University announced the undergraduate curriculum transformation. This meant redesigning all majors and degrees including the BA (Media and Communications) and the Digital Cultures major, and the introduction of the Bachelor of Advanced Studies. Motivated by a desire to blend the two recently merged programs, the department determined that Digital Cultures students would take first year Media and Communications units, and Media and Communications students would take Digital Cultures 2000 level units. Unfortunately, this meant MECO students could no longer major in Digital Cultures. By 2019, this arrangement was nixed by the deputy vice-chancellor (Education), and MECO students could once again major in Digital Cultures.

Since 2019, MECO and Digital Cultures have become more differentiated. New units in both programs address different dimensions of digital media. MECO introduced the very popular Open Learning unit OLES2017: Digital Influence through Social Media, which attracts over 700 students from across the University each semester. This filled a gap in the curriculum on social media for both Digital Cultures and MECO students. In 2020, MECO2604: Telling Stories with Data was introduced, which gives MECO students an understanding of digital methods in journalism. In 2021, Digital Cultures introduced a new first year unit ARIN1001: The Past and Futures of Digital Cultures, providing students in the major with a better grounding in the interdisciplinary formation of digital cultures. And in 2023, a second first year unit, ARIN1010: Elements of Digital Cultures, was introduced. These two units replace the two MECO units in the first year of the major.

MECO and Digital Cultures: disciplines and identities a decade later

The year is 2021, and the Digital Cultures program is thriving within MECO, expanding its number of academic staff, growing its unit offerings, and seeing significant growth in student enrolments at postgraduate and undergraduate levels. In 2016, there were fewer than 1,000 enrolments in Digital Cultures ARIN units. In 2021, there were nearly 3,000. Humphry and Marcus Carter joined the department as continuing staff in early 2017, and Olga Boichak and Mark Johnson followed in late 2019. In 2021, Terry Flew joined the program after a distinguished career at Queensland University of Technology, and in 2022 Joanne Gray joined the team, followed by Ben Egliston in 2023. Many synergies between Digital Cultures and MECO remain in both teaching and research.

The Centre for Digital Technologies and Societies, approved by the University in 2023, brings these fields together around the themes of: Platforms, Artificial Intelligence and Digital Cultures; Engaging Publics in a Digital Age; Digital Policy and Governance; and Global Storytelling and Digital Media. Affiliated to the new centre are existing nodes of expertise around the Sydney Games & Play Lab and the Computational Social Sciences Lab. The Digital Cultures research cluster has regular monthly meetings that feature research projects from academic staff, higher degree students

Figure 4.2 Terry Flew, 2022, photo by the Headshot Guys

and invited Australian and international researchers. Digital Cultures is a powerhouse in research into technology and culture, with its staff having published over 150 publications between them over the past five years. They've published in journals such as *New Media and Society*; *Convergence*; *Media, War and Conflict*; *International Journal of Social Robotics*; *Games and Culture*; *International Gambling Studies*; and even *Zoo Biology*.

The year is 2021, and a growing number of universities around the world are building programs like Digital Cultures. Hot topics in the field include the power of platforms, big data, artificial intelligence and bias, autonomous decision-making, smart city and smart home, social robotics, non-human technology users, digital media at war, streaming media, games, virtual reality and infrastructure politics. Digital Cultures has become an integral part of MECO, making sense of the role of technology in our mediatised social reality.

5
In search of a place to call home: MECO buildings

Chris Gillies

"Dominic, I think we need to get people out of here now!" Fiona Martin is recalling the time water began streaming down the back wall of a Holme Building radio lab during a class Dominic Santangelo was teaching.

It's one of many stories Martin shared as we talked via Zoom in June 2021. Sydney had just entered a second COVID-induced lockdown, and I was trying to find out about the buildings MECO has inhabited over its 20-year history. As we settled into conversation, two recurring themes emerged: building leaks and the department's shifts from "one jerry-rigged joint to the next jerry-rigged joint". I got the sense the department has been couch surfing while it has looked for a place to call home.

When Catharine Lumby arrived on campus in 1999 to begin designing the MECO program, she had an office on the top level of the RC Mills Building. It is a pale yellow bungalow style building with textured walls, tree ferns and a subterranean floor. Lumby and her colleagues worked from there until around 2003, when they moved down to the basement level. When the basement reached capacity, new staff had to be housed in other buildings.

In 2008, when Martin joined MECO, she had an office in the Transient Building. Built in 1948, the Transient was a temporary, shed-like, post-war construction erected to meet the needs of an influx of ex-military students who'd been encouraged into tertiary education by the government. Almost 70 years on from its construction and shortly following its demolition, the *South Sydney Herald* labelled it the University's ugliest building. The staid grey building, opposite RC Mills on the fig-tree-lined Fisher Road near the University's City Road entrance, was coming to an end, albeit with a garish flourish.

"While I was there, the faculty did up the building with new furniture in primary colours to make it more liveable," Martin recalled, "but it needed demolishing." Colleagues from Linguistics, who were also located in the building, joked that it had only survived because it was heritage listed. The health hazard its asbestos walls posed, however, could not be ignored, and it was torn down in December 2015 to make way for much-needed greenspace behind Eastern Avenue.

In 2009, all MECO academics moved to the Holme Building, next to the Footbridge Theatre. "Our offices were in a little nook below the level where the Holme Courtyard Café now stands," Martin said, "and we accessed them via a gate and walkway next to the front of the Footbridge Theatre." They celebrated the new space with a "housewarming" on 22 April 2009.

Tim Dwyer told me Holme was nicknamed "Westpac" in a nod to the corporate style offices that were built for MECO there. Dwyer, who also joined MECO in 2008, moved to Holme from the John Woolley Building, where he had been the sole MECO academic. He remembers staff were happy to

5 In search of a place to call home

Figure 5.1 RC Mills Building, 2024, photo by Fiona Wolf

finally be together in one place, but the traffic of Parramatta Road made it a noisy space to be in. Moreover, the Holme offices on the ground floor were very dark.

After successful lobbying by Anne Dunn, two radio labs and a teaching studio were built in the basement of Holme. This space had once been used as dressing rooms and storage for the Footbridge Theatre. The radio equipment was removed in 2017, but good acoustics and soundproofing mean it remains an excellent site for voiceover recording. The new labs and studio complemented the Education Building's TV studio, built in 2005, but they were problematic due to after-hours access difficulties and the inevitable water leaks during heavy rain, as experienced in Santangelo's class. Martin recalls the corridor to the labs reeked like a shearing shed full of wet wool.

Inside stories

Figure 5.2 Transient Building, photo courtesy of the University of Sydney

On its tenth birthday, MECO was together under one roof for the first time, but before dust had settled on the move the department had outgrown its space. It needed room for the Digital Media Unit (DMU), which had been created in 2011 to service student equipment requirements and was operating out of the Brennan MacCallum Building (see Chapter 6). MECO also needed to accommodate a merge with the Digital Cultures program (see Chapter 4) whose staff were housed on the third floor of John Woolley. Soon, a campaign was underway to move MECO to John Woolley, and in January 2014, with the support of then head of school Annamarie Jagose and with a lot of work behind the scenes, the department moved from Holme into the newly renovated second floor of the grand

5 In search of a place to call home

Figure 5.3 Holme Building, 2024, photo by Fiona Wolf

John Woolley Building. Dwyer said most staff embraced the move, recognising the department needed more space both for staff and teaching – and because of the traffic noise. The move would also provide MECO with a then state-of-the-art seminar room for meetings, conferences and seminars.

"The seminar room, S226, had all the technology needed for a media and communications department and it was nicely fitted out, so it had a pretty good vibe," Dwyer said, "But its usage became somewhat contentious as it proved popular with others within the school and the University."

Phil Glen, head of the DMU, told me the move brought an opportunity for staff across the department to have the informal chats that happen when you bump into someone in a corridor or lunchroom. He said having staff from across the department in one place meant they could finally share

Figure 5.4 John Woolley Building Level 2 entrance, 2022, photo by Maria Barbagallo

ideas and have conversations that were lost when split across different buildings.

The John Woolley Building is steeped in history. It is named after John Woolley, who became the University's first principal in 1852. The building is maze-like, which I experienced in March 2019 when walking the corridors on the first day of a Creative Non-Fiction class. I'd not stepped foot into a lecture theatre in 20 years and was recovering from significant surgery, but I was transfixed. The building smelt of books and hummed to the tune of creativity. Unseen were its hidden engineering features that over time had been closed-up or reshaped, facts I learned after talking to Glen. He told me of hidden tunnels and water tanks that once tested the winged keel that won Australia the America's Cup in 1983. As I learned from Martin, MECO too contributed to this reconfiguration with its specific technical needs.

5 In search of a place to call home

"Over $1.7 million of renovation work was done on the John Woolley to accommodate our growing program's needs," Martin said. "For the first time we had a purpose-built seminar room for our research presentations, an administrative office, offices for the DMU and space for tutors and visiting scholars." Students from other parts of the University gravitated to the wide, quiet corridor space and comfortable chairs.

However, the move into the building was not without its problems. The rooms nearest the kitchen leaked severely during the heavy rains of 2015 and flooded several times. There was also trouble with leaks from the air-conditioning, which was installed to keep staff computers cool. When other staff from the upper floors heard about the air-conditioning installation, which they had previously been denied due to the building's heritage listing, they campaigned for it to be introduced to the whole building. When that was approved in 2018, the building had to be vacated for three months while the work was done.

Within a few years of the move, MECO again outgrew its space. The merge with Digital Cultures and subsequent curriculum development saw the department expand further to become the second biggest revenue earner within the Faculty of Arts and Social Sciences. Now, MECO staff are scattered over several areas on two levels of John Woolley and the DMU is servicing labs in the Education Building and the Old Teachers' College, which from 2020 has housed the Sydney College of the Arts.

One of the ongoing problems MECO faces is that its chase for space over the past two decades has never fully satisfied MECO's production and computer lab needs. Dwyer told me of the difficulty finding teaching space for students. He remembers timetables that offered a space on the Camden campus – a rural suburb 65 kilometres southwest of the Sydney CBD.

Martin also recalled the difficulty, pointing out that MECO delivers a suite of popular programs that has grown consistently over two decades. "Meanwhile the University has been moving us from one jerry-rigged joint to the next jerry-rigged joint with all sorts of consequences, but never really catching up to our continual expansion."

When she arrived, labs were spread between the Transient, Holme, Education and Brennan MacCallum buildings. Significant planning was undertaken to overcome the haphazard nature of the production unit labs, and new purpose-designed teaching spaces were built in Brennan MacCallum. However, there was one flaw: no lifts were available to enable heavy equipment to be installed in the labs. Instead, DMU staff had to use the stairs to install the equipment whenever the studios were in use.

The Brennan MacCallum Building had other problems. Martin said the air-conditioning in the MECO LS120 lab never worked properly, creating a sense of suffocation that required teachers to leave the door open. This set off the alarm, which was eventually deactivated. The area was also subject to flooded corridors and subsequent evacuations.

From the beginning of the DMU, Glen has led the charge to create a media precinct in the Education Building, with a new radio lab, Mac computer labs, and eventually a VR lab and a 4K video lab.

Martin said the University has been grappling with its 170-year-old history that gifted it with heritage buildings, built during times when disability access and climate change were not considered. Part of the University's response needs to be new buildings and facilities that can adapt to its future needs.

5 In search of a place to call home

Looking to the future of MECO, student numbers are expected to keep growing, and with them the need for more staff and specialised space that can facilitate teaching in a rapidly changing media environment – not least marked by the pressure social media has placed on how we traditionally consume media. The challenge becomes figuring out how to teach with these pressures in buildings that were constructed during a different time and need significant renovation work to bring them in line with MECO's needs.

I learned that informal discussions began in 2019, with staff talking about what the bricks and mortar would need to look like to accommodate preparing graduates for the changing needs of the media industry, as well as the more mundane dilemma of where to house everyone now and in the future.

Ideas floated so far include the refurbishment of buildings familiar to MECO: John Woolley, Brennan MacCallum and the Education Building. This option, however, does not give the department the permanent home it requires, given the buildings' physical constraints. A second idea has been to commission a purpose-built building that would house MECO and the School of Economics. The benefit of this option is that it would give the school a strong identity and place on campus, and provide it with a building that caters for its specific needs and facilitates the teaching of graduates in a changing media landscape.

When I asked for her view on a new building, Martin said that as it stands now, MECO needs access to at least 21 teaching labs, including specialist facilities such as television and radio studios, VR creation and research spaces. She argued that it's time for the University to invest in a purpose-built MECO building in response to a globalising digital communications and media landscape, and a new home that reflects the department's economic contribution to the faculty.

Martin goes further, teasing out the idea that a new building is also an opportunity to reshape the school around what Terry Flew has described as the making of culture and cultural production.

The COVID-19 pandemic cooled these discussions, as the tertiary sector faced difficult times with fears of a drop in international student numbers and the looming prospect of tighter budgets. For now, 20 years on, the expanding discipline is still couch surfing.

6
"The glue that holds MECO together": Digital Media Unit
Alexandra Spence

The Digital Media Unit (DMU) was formed in 2011 to service the growing practical and technical needs of MECO and the School of Literature, Art and Media (SLAM). Previously, these needs had been met by Arts Digital, which operated at a faculty level, but the model needed to adapt to an increasing demand for more hands-on learning. In Arts Digital, MECO was supported by Adrian Langker, Daragh Lane and Justin Flynn, and later David Fay. Stephen Lambrinos managed this section.

A small advisory group, led by Steven Maras, came up with the design and staffing model of the DMU. Philip Glen was part of this group, brought on board because of his experience servicing the technical needs of the Journalism department at Charles Sturt University. Glen recalled that the DMU started out as a modest affair with facilities spread across the University, including a "tiny loans room", now referred to as "the old, old loans store", in the Brennan MacCallum Building. It operated with just four staff: Jacob Craig working in audio, Michael McCarthy (and shortly after Maria

Barbagallo) working in video, Marc Fernando working in IT and Glen managing the unit. Richard Manner, a technical officer for Theatre and Performance Studies, also worked closely with the DMU from its inception.

When the DMU started, it was supporting four undergraduate subjects and two postgraduate courses annually. A decade later (at the time of writing in 2021), the DMU is supporting around 13 units a year and operating a slew of new facilities. Glen's team also has doubled in size, with Barbagallo and Fernando joined by Shelagh Stanton, Josh Dowton, Mario Brce and Alexandra Spence. The once modest affair is now thriving and instrumental to the MECO program. As Blue Lucine, a documentary filmmaker who has been teaching at MECO since 2019 and who coordinates multiple media production units, put it, the DMU is "the glue that holds MECO together".

From the outset, the DMU mandate has been to offer a technical production stream to run alongside the theoretical underpinning of the MECO program. As Glen explained, the fundamental aim has been for practitioners to supply direct support to units of study, to form relationships with students and allow students to learn by doing. Furthermore, the DMU has "provide[d] an environment where doing is possible without requiring a skills uptake of the current faculty and staff".

Over the last decade, interest in the technical elements of MECO programs has grown immensely, and new units, such as podcasting, have seen huge enrolments. This growth has been fuelled by the increasing role of technology within society, including the affordability of professional-level consumer technology and the rising trend of YouTubers and podcasters.

The increased demand for these units has meant an increased demand for practical assistance from the DMU.

Another impetus for growth and change within the DMU came from the Sydney College of the Arts (SCA) merging with the Faculty of Arts and Social Sciences (FASS) at the end of 2019. This saw the DMU loans store amalgamate with the SCA loans store, gaining both the technical equipment and the expertise of Brce, the SCA loans store officer.

Brce explained that "the DMU maintains the culture of two schools across a unified team". Despite the initial growing pains – such as restructuring real estate to accommodate the additional loans gear, and learning and developing a new software program to monitor loans, facilities, and gear from both schools – the merge has been advantageous. Purchasing resources has become more streamlined, and resources can be pooled, such as the recent batch of GH5 cameras selected to service both media and SCA students.

The diversification and further specialisation have strengthened the DMU. "Having those smarts and those brains all in the one room, virtually or what have you, in the end game has to be positive," said Brce. "I think it's very useful to just be able to turn around to Rich or Maria, or anyone else in the room, and immediately grab onto specialist knowledge."

Brce is referring to Richard Manner, who manages and services SLAM's Rex Cramphorn Studio. Although Manner's main priority is within Theatre and Performance Studies, he regularly interfaces with the DMU and generously offers his expertise and workshop facilities to assist with the repair of broken DMU equipment.

The DMU also has a strong alliance with the FASS Media Room, which was developed in 2017 in response to the growing need for a facility to assist with the creation of online

Figure 6.1 A broadcast exercise in Semester 2, 2023, photo by Mikhaila Jurkiewicz

educational material. The Media Room was designed by Glen, alongside the Social Sciences Building architects and ICT AV team. Jacob Craig – one of the DMU's first employees – designed the room's refurbishment and now services it, along with Tyler Mahoney.

The loans store operates in the John Woolley Building. The DMU technicians maintain close relationships with MECO and SCA academics to ensure they are sourcing the technical devices and equipment needed for each unit. But utilising high-level technology is not a requirement for making meaningful content, and in contemporary media and communications industries even mobile phones can be used to create impactful content. "Students at Sydney University learn to make meaningful communication rather than only learning

6 "The glue that holds MECO together"

about technology and how to use the big gear," Glen said. Accordingly, the DMU provides everything from affordable consumer devices to high-end cameras.

The loans store also functions as a place where students and staff can go to gain tech support, advice and consultation. Glen explained, "The strength of the DMU is that an academic can walk down the hall and go, 'I have an idea to do this thing, can we?' and we go, 'Well, let's have a think about it', propose a solution and go from there."

Stanton also appreciates the student interactions that occur at the store. "Every year there's one or two [students] that turn up a lot, borrow heaps of stuff, have a chat, ask for little favours and build a bit more of a relationship, which is really nice."

Lucine has experienced this first-hand. "I know I can always count on them to bounce ideas off and that they'll work with me to find the best solution to problems. They make time to explain things to students, and I know that I can trust them with providing hands-on support. I always say, 'Go see the DMU, they'll help you!'"

In addition to the loans store, the DMU also consists of audio podcasting, TV broadcasting and VR spaces located in the Education Building. Again, the DMU's own officers – Glen and Stanton – played a large role in the design and build of these spaces, and they are serviced predominantly by Stanton and Barbagallo. This has resulted in what Brce described as a "continuous line of thought" from conception to development to practice. Stanton and Barbagallo also spend time in these learning spaces with students. As Barbagallo said, "In the early days we didn't have the time, so we weren't called upon to provide technical support in class – akin to a tutor. It's developed more that way, and I think it's a wonderful

Figure 6.2 Phil Glen and Shelagh Stanton filming and recording at the ANZCA conference in 2017, photo courtesy of Maria Barbagallo

opportunity to pass on the knowledge you gain being a technical officer."

The main podcasting studio was built in 2018, replacing a space in the Holme Building that had been used for audio work. The studio is booked for all the podcasting classes at both undergraduate and postgraduate level, and students can also access the studio independently. Initially built by Stanton to cater for MECO's news bulletin and radio broadcasting courses, it has since been adapted to service the recent coursework move towards podcasting and post-production. As such, it consists of a broadcasting desk connected to the classroom next door and has podcasting microphones that allow for up to three guests to be interviewed at once.

The main facility for visual media is the TV broadcast studio and its associated vision switching room, audio mixing room and server room. Part of Barbagallo's role is to prepare the TV studio for timetabled classes, to offer production support, and to ensure proper work health and safety standards are adhered to. Barbagallo explained that the TV studio offers students experience reading news, operating cameras, doing autocues and switching. She commented on the boom that TV broadcast has seen during COVID-19 and said she thinks "if anything it's going to become more prominent".

One of the newest facilities for the DMU is the Mixed Realities Lab, which is commonly referred to as the VR lab. The new lab, proposed by Fiona Martin and Gerard Goggin, was built in 2019 with the assistance of VR researcher Marcus Carter. It consists of a studio space with 20 high-end PCs and Oculus VR headsets, and a podcasting voiceover booth with an iMac computer, Rodecaster and microphones. It also has a VR cave – a 3 metre by 3 metre regulation space designed with a computer cupboard flush to the wall – enabling the whole space to be used for "room scale" VR. As Carter explained, "Rather than focusing just on facilities that support VR content, the MECO VR lab is designed to facilitate group discussion between students after experiencing VR content. The hope is that this will provide new opportunities for educators to incorporate VR into their classes, across the faculty."

When it was commissioned, the VR lab was regarded as one of the best of its kind. Although it has yet to be used to its full advantage due to COVID-19 and restricted campus access, it's a very promising space for the future direction of MECO and the DMU.

Inside stories

Figure 6.3 A broadcast exercise in Semester 2, 2023, photo by Mikhaila Jurkiewicz

In addition to the physical spaces and equipment loans, an integral component of the DMU is IT support. Fernando has been the DMU's IT officer since 2012. He administers several computer systems used by MECO units and works with ICT to get the software and hardware set up, tested and supported for the MECO computer labs. Working alongside MECO academics, he helps to maintain the blogs used for specific units and assists with some of the publishing platforms used for research, industry–student engagement and outreach.

The DMU has also offered AV and IT support for various SLAM awards ceremonies, conferences and even SLAM Christmas parties, though these events have been put on hold since the start of the COVID-19 pandemic in early 2020.

6 "The glue that holds MECO together"

During the pandemic, the DMU was unable to run as usual and had to shift its focus to support online learning. Because the DMU has such a close relationship with MECO, the DMU is often the first point of call before the University's ICT central services. As such, the DMU had to quickly adjust to offer remote technical assistance. Numerous USB microphones were bought and mailed out to the homes of teaching staff and students to support ad hoc remote teaching and learning. Craig refurbished the TV broadcast studio to accommodate a HyFlex learning environment, and the space was heavily used for webinars. The DMU changed the structure of the booking system to ensure there was enough time between in-person visits. It was also necessary to find alternative routes to obtain equipment, as international shipping had slowed down and some factories in Italy had stopped working altogether, meaning some gear was simply unavailable.

Furthermore, the timing of the pandemic aligned with the SCA merger, which made the adjustment and amalgamation trickier than anticipated. The DMU had to learn to triage, gauging, as Brce said, "what's important now and what's important later".

As the DMU looks ahead, one of the most pressing needs is for more space. They also think it is essential to continue self-designing their facilities – something previously outsourced to private contractors. As Stanton explained, "We know what we need and if we continue to design and build our own spaces, then we can maintain and adapt to these needs." They plan to hire more loans store staff, which would free up Stanton and Barbagallo to address the more specific needs of maintenance, supervision and demonstration within the various studios. The wish list also includes hiring a VR studio technician to maintain and assist in the VR spaces on an active basis; overhauling some facilities, such as installing new flooring and redesigned acoustics within the TV studio; and developing a critical listening lounge with spatialised audio for the podcasting and audio media students.

If the trajectory of the last decade is anything to go by, the future of the DMU promises even more diversification and expansion. As Glen said, "We've got to keep widening our skill set, and keep that going into the future."

7
Imparting wisdom: journalists teaching journalism

Tim Piccione

"I managed to pull a rabbit out of a hat," Pam Walker explains, sitting up in her chair. She is recounting the time she chased down a lead that won her a Fairfax Best News Story award in 1998, the first of four during her career. "I've probably mentioned it in class," she says. I do, in fact, recall the yarn. I heard it in a 2019 tutorial as one of her MECO6900: News Writing students. Not content to hand in the same copy as every other reporter who attended the press conference announcing contracts for the Howard government's Job Services privatisation, Walker followed up on the rumour that a multimillion dollar deal was given to somebody with no office or staff. She asked for contact details and, to her surprise, received them. She asked for interviews and, again, received them. Nearing her deadline, Walker found the man and discovered he was simply farming the contract back out and adding his 10 percent cut. The man agreed to do an interview and have his photo taken. The next day, "the member of Parliament, Janice Crosio, walked in [to the Lower House] waving our paper," she recalls. "The entire day in

Figure 7.1 Bunty Avieson and Pam Walker with the students participating in the first MECO Newsroom, 2019, photo courtesy of Pam Walker

Parliament was on that story." The controversy dominated the news cycle for over a week, and the contract was later reassigned.

Walker uses the experience as an example to push students past their comfort zone to find the best possible story. "I teach students to put their neck out a little bit, to take risks, not to be afraid of people saying no, not to be afraid of rejection, and to make sure they have a plan B so that if plan A doesn't work, they can go to something else."

MECO's success in teaching future journalists can be attributed in part to the passion that Walker and her colleagues share. For staff with a collective wealth of experience in

7 Imparting wisdom

television, radio, podcasting, newspapers and magazines, stories like Walker's are an inevitable and appreciated part of the classroom experience, alongside theory and practical exercises.

"You know, one of the most fantastic things about working in the media is that you do get this front-row seat to what's really going on in a country," Bunty Avieson tells me. Avieson is a MECO journalism lecturer who worked in Bhutan, funded by the United Nations, from 2008 to 2009. She consulted for the *Bhutan Observer* newspaper, which had recently launched, and Reporters Without Borders. It's this, watching first-hand the building of a new democracy, that she considers her most rewarding experience as a media professional.

When I ask the other lecturers about rewarding professional experiences, their faces light up. "One of my greatest treasures is meeting Sir David Attenborough," Alison Ray, a broadcast journalism lecturer, tells me. She filmed a TV segment with the famed British broadcaster and recalls, "Everybody was walking around with a smile on their face that day." She continues with a highlight reel of her 30-year career as a television, video and radio journalist: doing a news bulletin while trapped in an elevator with Chris Isaak; watching Dave Grohl ride a Razor scooter around the ABC foyer; working on a documentary with two-time Academy Award winner Sir Peter Ustinov; and interviewing Bob Hope, Julie Andrews and Sir David Lean. Playful name dropping and digressions have been part of Ray's units since she joined MECO in 2010.

Lea Redfern, the department's audio and podcasting lecturer, counts two award-winning documentaries among her career standouts. The first, titled *A Place You Cannot Imagine*,

Figure 7.2 Bunty Avieson, 2022, photo by Bill Green

details the experience of refugees sent to immigration detention centres in the Australian desert. It won the 2003 Human Rights Radio Award from the Australian Human Rights Commission. The other is called *Almost Flamboyant* and won the inaugural Sarah Award for radio drama in New York in 2016. Redfern grins widely as she tells me it is about a "talking taxidermied flamingo". But it's not always about the accolades.

7 Imparting wisdom

Figure 7.3 Lea Redfern, 2019, photo by Sister Scout

Redfern also tells me how rewarding it was to work with ordinary people to crowd-source stories in the latter part of her 20-year ABC career.

Prior to these career-defining experiences, and long before these stories would be recounted to budding journalism students in a classroom, the educators had to crack their way into the industry. Redfern began at the ABC with a traineeship, which she admits must seem foreign to today's journalism students. The cross-media program trained university graduates in television, multimedia and radio. "My joke was that a lot of people who were starting were lying [because they said] they were interested in radio when they really just wanted to get on television," she recounts. "But I was the opposite, all I wanted to do was radio."

When Ray began working at the ABC in 1978, she was both the only female and the first University of Technology Sydney graduate to be accepted into a cadetship at the public broadcaster. After a year of training, she made her way through Channel Nine, Channel Ten and SBS, before heading to England and Granada Television where her one-day contract became a news editor position in just nine months. This was largely due to her work on the Manchester air disaster in August 1985, which left 55 people dead. "I got to work at 7:00 am and at 7:13 am, all the police scanners, everything went dead quiet for 15 seconds. I was in the newsroom, and then all hell broke loose," she says. "What was it like? Horrific, chaotic. Just absolutely horrific."

Working on the UK's *Sunday Express* the day of the Zeebrugge ferry disaster in March 1987, which left 193 passengers dead, was a similarly trying experience for Avieson. "Just shocking," she says. It was a far cry from her first journalism job at a Melbourne suburban newspaper, the *Mordialloc News*. She laughs, remembering the first professional story she wrote at the age of 19 about a 10-year-old boy who built a brick fence taller than himself for his mother. "I think I thought it was really important," she says. "I worked really, really hard on that story."

7 Imparting wisdom

For Walker, it came down to one important thing. "I always wanted to be a journalist," she says. "I discovered a passion. So, I did it." She got a foot in the door with a two-day fill-in position at the *Fairfield Champion* and remained in the industry for the next two decades, thanks to her tenacious work ethic and love for the field.

Like their different introductions into the field of journalism, all four found distinct pathways into university teaching. Avieson's time in Bhutan contributed to a book and a PhD, leading her into full-time academia. By 2010, tired of 4 am radio and 6 am television starts, Ray, who was running her own business, went looking for an extra day of work a week. Instead, successfully answering an online ad, she was given "open slather" to create a MECO curriculum directly informed by her storied career. After balancing different editor jobs with part-time teaching at the University of Western Sydney, the University of Technology Sydney, the University of New South Wales and the University of Sydney, Walker started full-time teaching in 2018. Leaving the ABC, Redfern came to the University of Sydney in 2017 to teach undergraduate podcasting, an evolving curriculum she immediately updated.

After decades of practical experience, these seasoned media professionals are now tasked with teaching aspiring journalists and crafting curriculums, working alongside colleagues with a range of professional backgrounds and academic skill sets.

After joining the department in 2005, Megan Le Masurier directed the Master of Publishing and coordinated MECO3606: Media Production: Advanced Media Writing. Before that, she worked as a journalist and editor in the Australian magazine industry for two decades, including stints as deputy editor for *ELLE Australia* and editor for

Countdown. Le Masurier's PhD on *Cleo* magazine, supervised by Catharine Lumby, strengthened feminist media studies in the discipline. Moreover, Le Masurier was one of the international pioneers of slow media studies, a new form of research which has sought to challenge the news media's fascination with speed by returning to issues of memory and the "recovery of attention".

As Steven Maras recounts, Le Masurier was an incredibly patient and generous editor and interlocutor for MECO students, introducing them to different styles of writing. At a time when student consultations were infrequent, Megan always had a queue of students lined up outside her office door. Her ethics of care for students was exemplified in the work she voluntarily undertook to provide them with clear guidelines on academic integrity and avoiding plagiarism. She was central to the success of magazine studies in the Master of Publishing and in the teaching of Adobe InDesign to postgraduate students. Together with Fiona Giles, she also championed feature journalism in the department and nurtured entire cohorts of students to find their voices. She was especially influential on the students who did international internships and those who were up to the challenge of sourcing stories with a fresh angle.

Journalist, author and educator Benedetta Brevini's current teaching is in the political economy of communication and technology, and in communication and the environment. Joining MECO in 2013, she still collaborates with and contributes to outlets including *South China Morning Post, The Conversation, The Guardian* and *openDemocracy*.

Fiona Martin's media career began in 1987, working for stations like 2SER, 2WEB, ABC Radio National and ABC Radio Sydney, first on news and features, and later news talk

7 Imparting wisdom

and documentary. An award-winning feature maker, she produced the ABC's first regional cross-platform documentary and ground-breaking programs on women online. Joining MECO in 2008 after a decade at Southern Cross University, Martin has overseen the digital transformation of MECO's journalism teaching. She created the department's postgraduate MECO6925: Online Journalism unit and taught digital feature production to undergraduates in MECO3602: Online Media. She introduced the department's first ongoing blogs: *Salience*, the journalism showcase, and *Parallax*, documenting MECO's overseas journalism fellowships. She now teaches the final year industry innovation research unit.

Penny O'Donnell drew on extensive academic and professional media experience in Latin America when she revitalised MECO6926: International Media Practice. Her students say studying global media breaks down stereotypes, broadens their worldview and teaches them diverse ways of creating media and news narratives. Additionally, O'Donnell has worked with colleagues on several Australian Research Council-funded projects and produced findings that have enabled MECO journalism students to better understand and engage with the changing contours of media and journalism work across a wide range of contexts and cultures. This has included investigations into the future of Australian newspapers and into job loss in journalism both in Australia and across the Global North–South divide.

Margaret Van Heekeren joined MECO in 2017 after nearly 20 years as a newspaper, radio and television journalist and over a decade working at Charles Sturt University. She now coordinates and lectures in first year undergraduate media units and recently developed the data journalism unit MECO2604: Telling Stories with Data. Van Heekeren also

Figure 7.4 Fiona Martin, 2012, photo courtesy of the University of Sydney

runs MECO6913: Public Opinion, Policy and Public Sphere, a postgraduate theory unit that she says, "emphasises the roundness of MECO degrees, which encourage students not just to 'do' but to also understand the media and communications environment".

All the educators I spoke with seem to agree with this notion that places equal value on teaching practical aspects of journalism alongside critical thinking skills – doing as well as understanding.

7 Imparting wisdom

Figure 7.5 Penny O'Donnell, 2022, photo courtesy of the University of Sydney

"I think the real-world experience helps you to know that there is always an interaction between the practical and the theoretical," says Redfern. "You can have all the great ideas in the world, but if you don't record it properly and it doesn't sound good for audio, then you're not doing yourself or the people you're working with any favours."

Figure 7.6 Margaret Van Heekeren, 2022, photo by Bill Green

For Ray, teaching Sydney's next television and video journalists became a calling to improve the quality of reporting and storytelling on our airwaves. "The last newsroom I worked in, I saw so much s—t passing as television news, that by the time I got to Sydney University I was determined that I would teach people how to report properly and not just come

7 Imparting wisdom

up with the dodgiest crap to fill a hole," she says, with an unapologetic conviction I came to know well as one of her students.

Ray insists that those who report the news and influence public opinion need, foremost, to be decent and empathetic people.

According to Avieson, the department can't only teach students how to be journalists; students also need a bigger perspective and critical understanding of the media landscape. That's the difference, she explains, between vocational training (a J-school) and university education: learning how to write a story, conduct an interview, produce professional content and then appreciate where those skills sit within the media more broadly. "You understand what those issues are, whose voices are missing, and who's holding power in that structure."

Indeed, critically analysing the media landscape is a crucial part of journalism. And it is likely more important than ever in the age of fake news, social media algorithms, false equivalence and the 24-hour news cycle.

"At the beginning of each semester I say to students that this course aims to do two things: teach you how to be a creator of news, but also teach you how to be a consumer of news," says Walker. "We have to teach critical thinking and make students aware that everything they see on social media or that they hear somewhere is not necessarily true. I make them suspicious."

It's clear from these conversations that the combination of theory and practice within MECO's journalism units is motivated by a desire to send well-rounded, analytical and ethical journalists into the media workforce. "That's what I love about it, is that we can give people skills that are really useful, but we can also give them a theoretical framework that will challenge the way they think," says Redfern. "That is such a gift that universities give."

These educators are just a small portion of the experienced journalists on the MECO faculty. They provided more stories on the joys of their professional careers than I could fit into this chapter. There's an entire book's worth of anecdotes sitting inside MECO's John Woolley Building. Emotional highs and lows, career-defining stories and projects, and laughter thinking back on how it all started – each experience, good or bad, has had a clear and direct influence on how they teach and pass down knowledge.

"Do I miss it? I loved it while I did it," says Avieson. "I loved the energy and knowing what goes on behind closed doors. But actually miss it day to day, not so much."

I get the sense that transitioning into teaching was the ideal way to remain in an industry they each love, while also being in a position to impact its future. Like the story Walker tells her students about always having a backup strategy for success, each of these accomplished journalists found a way into the rewarding second phase of their careers: a plan B. Although in this case, plan B was not because plan A failed, but because it succeeded.

8
Teaching undergraduate students to question, to innovate ... and to push back

Cheryl O'Byrne and Cindy Cameronne

On 13 October 2014, Penny O'Donnell woke to find herself on the front page of *The Australian's* Higher Education section. "Uni degrees in indoctrination", read the headline. The article accused O'Donnell, along with a media professor at the University of Technology Sydney, of "indoctrinating students, not educating them". *The Australian's* media editor, Sharri Markson, claimed they were unfairly influencing students to be biased against News Corporation Ltd, owned by Rupert Murdoch.[1]

O'Donnell had given a lecture that asked students of MECO1002: Media and Communications Landscapes to consider the inordinate power News Corp wields and questioned whether this power was in the public interest. Unbeknownst to her, Markson had attended her lecture "undercover", posing as a student, and recorded the class.

"It was potentially a job losing moment," O'Donnell says.

---

1   For the full story, see O'Donnell & Hutchinson, 2015.

But that was not the end of the story for the journalism lecturer or her students.

"What ended up happening," O'Donnell remembers, "was that there was a big sort of Twitter storm around it."

O'Donnell's students, in their first year of media studies, pushed back against the narrative on social media and in op-eds.

Students poked fun at the idea of Markson going undercover in their classes. Nick Stoll tweeted: "Have put in a request for Markson to do my essays for me as an 'undercover' student. You know, because I'm brainwashed."

They also pointed out the hypocrisy in accusing the University of bias. Alex McKinnon tweeted: "Looking for some media bias? Here's the Premier of New South Wales starring in an ad for *The Daily Telegraph*". Lane Sainty also wrote an op-ed in *Honi Soit* titled "Bit rich for The Oz to cry indoctrination".

Students were offended at being characterised as brainwashed and unable to think for themselves about how the media worked.

"Within three days," says O'Donnell, "the whole issue was totally transformed from the University of Sydney brainwashing its students to the pushback of the media students saying 'what you're talking about is rubbish. We know what we want in the media and we are going to do it.'"

While O'Donnell doesn't believe her students' pushback changed Markson's mind, she knows it had an extraordinary impact on the students' learning.

"You're probably not going to remember that lecture we had in five years' time," she told her students, "but what you will remember is that when the newspaper attacked you for being brainwashed, you turned around and said, 'No, that's not true.' And you set about creating a new narrative about your own position as future media contributors. That's something that'll stay with you for the rest of your lives."

This wasn't a planned part of the curriculum, but O'Donnell couldn't have designed anything that captures the degree's tenets more elegantly. Ironically, given Markson's intention, the stunt showcased that MECO undergraduate students are learning to be critical, independent thinkers. They are learning through a combination of theory and practice. They are learning within a program that has a deep connection to industry. And they are learning to be active participants in the media ecosystem. All of this has been true since the degree's inception more than 20 years ago, and it remains so today.

Catharine Lumby points out a further irony: that Markson had herself been a MECO student at the University of Sydney in 2002 and 2003. Lumby remembers her as a highly engaged and extremely capable student.

For Lumby, the claims that Media and Communications degrees are largely taught by Marxist-leaning academics who teach students to be hostile to the profession date back to a campaign in the late 90s by conservative media commentator Keith Windschuttle who launched multiple attacks on the teaching of journalism along the same lines. "It is one strand in the long running so-called culture wars. But in my experience, it is a total or at least very dated fantasy to imagine that the vast majority of Media and Communications scholars are interested in 'brainwashing' their students. In my experience it is difficult to get undergraduate students to do anything except challenge their lecturers' ideas. And that's exactly as it should be."

Lumby notes that the whole ethos of MECO is grounded in valuing professional skills along with critical thinking skills and that the first two academics who designed the four-year degree, herself and Anne Dunn, were both people with long and successful careers as print and broadcast journalists. Proof of that focus, Lumby says, is a 1999 article in *The Australian* on her appointment to launch the new degree. It is headlined "Industry Link Stressed" and it quotes her as saying, "I want it to be the mission of this program to forge meaningful links with industry, to involve industry on advising on units of study, and to make the program responsive to training and retraining needs in the industry."

Lumby is also quoted as saying that, "In this degree, almost 50 percent of the media studies component – leaving aside the second arts major – is certainly oriented at teaching them professional skills. But those skills are always taught against a background of critical theory and a history of ideas. I think those two things have to work together."

Indeed, prospective students reading the 2000 Faculty of Arts Undergraduate Handbook found an "interdisciplinary degree which offers students professional training in media and communications and an advanced education in the history and theory of the field". The "professional training" element spans the fields of "print, radio, television, online media, and media relations" and students "explore these areas through a diverse array of disciplinary perspectives and relevant critical theories". Units of study focus on "media production and consumption, the structure of the media and communications industry, the media's role in culture and politics, the regulation of the media, and legal and public policy issues in the field". Over the four years, students would complete a Media and Communications major, an Arts or Economics second major,

8 Teaching undergraduate students to question

electives in the humanities (that could lead to a third major), a unit on textual analysis (cross-listed with English) and an internship in the media industry.

The degree remained under Lumby's leadership for its first six years. During this time, a teaching and researching team grew around her: Dunn, Geraint Evans, Kate Crawford, Richard Stanton, Marc Brennan, Fiona Giles and Steven Maras. Together, in addition to establishing the department's first postgraduate offerings, they expanded the undergraduate units of study, from two in 2000 to more than ten by 2007. In 2004, they began to offer the degree at both pass and honours levels. They also tweaked the degree nomenclature and structure: the Media and Communications element was no longer called a "major" – it was the essence of the degree; the internship moved from third to fourth year; and students could choose a major from a wider pool of areas, no longer limited to Arts or Economics.

Fiona Martin joined the undergraduate team in 2008, the same year that Lumby departed for UNSW. This was also the year MECO formalised its relationship with the Faculty of Law – present from the outset because its UAI was comparable to Law's – by implementing a combined specialist degree: BA (Media & Communications) and Bachelor of Laws.

Martin was undergraduate degree director from 2020 to 2021. When we ask her to compare the degree in 2008 to the degree in 2021, she tells us, "The degree hasn't changed enormously. The fundamentals of theory and practice are still there. And the cross talk between them." But the team, Martin continues, has adapted these fundamentals to an evolving media landscape. True to Lumby's word, the program has very much been responsive to industry needs.

Martin explains that the most significant drivers of change have been the digitisation of media content; the growth of the internet, web and mobile media; and the growth of social media and online communication platforms. In 2008, students following the original undergraduate degree trajectory did not learn much about internet theory or online media production until a third year MECO3602: Online Media unit. Now, however, digital media skills are embedded across the degree, rendering that unit obsolete. To some extent, all MECO units are now online media units. The department discontinued Online Media in 2018 and integrated some of its unique concepts into first and second year, including two new core units: MECO1004: Introduction to Media Production and a data journalism unit, MECO2604: Telling Stories with Data.

Media convergence also has meant that the department has increased the scope of what it teaches. From 2000, the handbook advertised a degree that spanned the fields of print, radio, television, online media and media relations; now, this has become "written news and feature journalism, audio, video, social media and public relations". These subtle changes represent a huge expansion of content across diverse platforms. *"Audio"*, for example, adds podcasting to radio; and *"video"* extends beyond television to augmented reality and TikTok. *"Social media"* did not exist when the degree began. When Martin arrived in 2008, Twitter was in its infancy; by 2014, students were using it to turn around Markson's narrative. O'Donnell and another MECO academic, Jonathon Hutchinson, studied the Twitter traffic after Markson's article and coined the term "pushback journalism" to describe how the students created original news content on social media to make their voices heard in the debate, exemplifying the "fifth estate" role of social media in holding mainstream media accountable.

The department has adapted its curriculum to ensure students are learning to dissect these new technologies and produce within them. At the same time, they have seen the need to ensure students understand what working within such an innovative, digitalised industry entails. In 2011, they introduced the core unit MECO1002: Digital Media and Communications Landscapes (since renamed Media 4.0: Work and Policy). Martin explains that this unit teaches students to look at the nature of media industries from a critical perspective. They need to explore questions that MECO students were not asking in the first decade of the degree, such as: How do you organise yourself to succeed as a creative worker in the era of precarious labour? What do platform analytics mean for you as a media practitioner? How do you counter mistrust and disinformation online? How do you interact safely and productively with audiences online?

Students are asking these questions in the context of careers that few – if any – of their earlier counterparts considered. Martin has noticed a decline in the number of graduates who are pursuing journalism and an increase in those working in communications and native content development. Many, for example, are working in agencies on social media campaigns, in trade industry newsrooms, as media liaisons, or as social media editors and community managers. Martin explains that MECO never was a J-school, but journalism did once have a more substantial share of the program's attention. Over the years, MECO's focus has become "more pluralised" as its academics "are seeing new fields of media and communications and digital cultures that our students can traverse".

Apart from the digital disruptions, the other major source of change for MECO undergraduates came from within the University. In 2016, Deputy Vice-Chancellor (Education) Pip Pattison presided over a University-wide restructure of undergraduate degrees. Sydney adopted the Melbourne Model, which favoured generalist, four-year undergraduate degrees and specialist, career-oriented postgraduate degrees. For most undergraduate degrees, which had been three years, this meant adding a year of Open Learning Environment and interdisciplinary units. For MECO, however, which was one of the few programs across the University that already had a four-year bachelor's degree, this meant losing units to make way for the new requirements.

Elizabeth Connor, the school administration manager, recalls there was "considerable argument against the change" at the time. Some four-year degrees that had "a professional bent" were allowed to retain their structure. Given this caveat, and MECO's established brand, the department argued strongly that it should be excluded from the change, but that was not to be. Under Annamarie Jagose, head of school at the time, MECO's undergraduate degree was altered to fit the new model.

Margaret Van Heekeren is the current undergraduate coordinator. When we ask her about the future of the degree, she echoes Martin's view, and Lumby's before her, that the essence of the degree will remain intact even as its edges are constantly in motion. "Our students," she observes, "learn not just 'how to' but also 'why'," and they are led by a team of academics who ensure the curriculum "stays abreast of industry trends. This combination of a theory/practice base and responsive curriculum has served it well for the past two decades of massive media transformation and will continue to do so in the future."

In Markson's 2014 article, a News Corp executive shares his "suspicion that journalism as it is taught and journalism as it is practised are two different things". He seems to intend this as a disparagement but, given the trajectory and values of the undergraduate MECO degree at the University of Sydney, we can take it as a commendation. Since Lumby started the degree, its caretakers have ensured students learn journalistic and other media industry practices. But it has never confined itself to vocational training. Alongside the practice, undergraduate students have been learning to question, to innovate ... and to push back.

Works cited

O'Donnell, P., & Hutchinson, J. (2015). Pushback journalism: Twitter, user engagement and journalism students' responses to "The Australian". *Australian Journalism Review, 37*(1), 105–20.

9
Story-making in a global context: the Master of Media Practice

Cheryl O'Byrne and Anna Jenica Bacud

Just as the first undergraduates were completing their degree, a new component of the MECO project was introduced: the Master of Media Practice (MMP). Like many master's degrees, its purpose was to offer a postgraduate option for practitioners who wanted to upgrade their skills and for others who wanted to add to their skill set ahead of a career change. In 2004, its first year, 146 students signed up. Most of these enrolled in the full MMP, with some opting for the Graduate Certificate or Graduate Diploma pathways. Approximately 60 percent were domestic students and 40 percent international.

Within two years, the number of enrolments more than doubled. They held steady for a decade, and by 2017 were climbing again, more than tripling between 2017 and 2021. In 2013, international enrolments began outpacing domestic enrolments, and in 2021, more than 92 percent of those enrolled in the MMP program were international students.

MMP is now the second most popular postgraduate coursework offering in the Faculty of Arts and Sciences (just

Inside stories

Figure 9.1 Intense focus as students polish their filming skills at an April 2016 presser, photo courtesy of Maria Barbagallo

behind Economics) with nearly 1,200 students. What accounts for this extraordinary rise?

From the outset, one of the most remarkable features of the degree has been the way it situates media production in a global context. Anne Dunn had extensive experience working across print, television and radio media in Australia and the UK prior to joining the academy. She drew on this worldview when she devised MECO6926: International Media Practice as one of the degree's four core units, which introduces postgraduate students to comparative study of media around the world. At a time when media education globally was predominantly Western-centric, Dunn's reading list included case studies on media in China, Ghana, Lebanon and Mexico, as well as France, Sweden, the UK and the USA.

In 2008, Penny O'Donnell joined MECO as a senior lecturer in international media and journalism and took over as coordinator of this unit. She had extensive experience in international media, having graduated with an MA (Social Communication) with Merit, from the Universidad Iberoamericana in Mexico City; gained expertise in professional news media at ABC Radio (Sydney), Notimex (Mexico City) and Coradep (Managua, Nicaragua); and engaged in collaborative teaching on reconciliation, social justice and human rights at the University of Technology Sydney. She adapted the unit curriculum to engage the increasing global diversity of international students enrolling in the MMP. O'Donnell wrote an article for *Synergy*, the Institute of Teaching and Learning's magazine, on the challenge of getting students to listen to each other and engage with unfamiliar or ideologically different points of view on global news issues. One student told her, "In the past, there was silence between us, now journalists are shouting at each other. Shouting is better than silence."

International Media Practice quickly became, and remains, popular with both domestic and international students. O'Donnell says it is to Dunn's credit that a review of the MMP, undertaken in 2017 by the Tertiary Education Quality and Standards Agency (TEQSA), concluded that a global media focus is a key part of what attracts the degree's large and increasing number of international students.

The global media focus extends beyond International Media Practice into other core units. MECO6902: Legal and Ethical Issues in Media Practice focuses on Australia but, as unit coordinator Tim Dwyer explains, students engage with the

Figure 9.2 Student prepares for a presser in May 2015, photo courtesy of Maria Barbagallo

material by comparing Australian media law, ethics, regulation and policies to American, European and Asian contexts. MECO6936: Social Media Communication, coordinated by Jonathon Hutchinson, emphasises the Southeast Asian digital communication environment and incorporates communication practices from First Nations peoples in Australia and other parts of the world.

Elective units also have a substantial global focus. One example is MECO6929: Chinese Media Studies in Global Contexts, coordinated by Joyce Nip. Another is MECO6925: Online Journalism. Unit coordinator Fiona Martin teaches this unit with "the aim of developing curiosity, empathy and cultural competence" in her students. To this end, she explains, "I encourage students to bring examples of compelling journalism from their own countries and cultures, and to talk about why it communicates effectively with different types of audiences." Martin invites students "to report on issues that affect their everyday lives, and so they cover topics like rent and wage exploitation of international students, working visa policy and application challenges, political surveillance and human rights abuses – even the ethics of adopting rescue pets on student visa".

Students in Alison Ray's elective MECO6924: Video and Television Journalism are also acting as citizen journalists. They are learning to research, shoot and edit video news stories using formats that are commonly recognised in Europe, the Americas, Asia and Australia. And, as Ray explains, students are using current 4K and HD production technology so they can "reflect on how their work fits within a broader international context of newsgathering and broadcast operations".

The TEQSA review highlighted another reason students have been attracted to the degree: the choices afforded them by the range of topics of study on offer. This was true in the degree's first decade and was consolidated by a curriculum overhaul that began in 2015.

From 2004 to 2014, MMP candidates were required to complete 48 credit points, including 24 credit points of core units (News Writing, Dealing with the Media, Legal and Ethical Issues in Media Practice, and International Media Practice) and 24 credit points of elective units. Students could choose from MECO electives on topics such as literary journalism, public relations, sports reporting, political journalism, broadcast journalism and online journalism. They could also opt for electives from other disciplines such as Asian Studies, Film Studies, the United States Studies Centre, and Gender and Cultural Studies. As the TEQSA review observed, students were learning that successful content creation was a combination of professional skills, media theory and the development of "political, social, cultural and economic perspectives of the kind that the media are responsible for presenting to the public".

Gang Shen was an MMP student during these early years. He completed the degree in 2010 and is currently the director of the media centre of the International Finance Forum, a China-based international organisation for financial communications. He tells us that the MMP taught him "the essential knowledge for future research in mass communications" and "embedded the most important values in [his] mind: pursuing facts and truth and always working for the interests of the people and society".

Victoria Ong graduated from the program in 2014. She highlights her internships, including one with Nine News that had her conducting vox pops in Sydney's CBD. Experiences like this developed the "skills and confidence to venture into the demanding world of broadcast journalism and eventually venture out on my own," Ong says. After nearly four years

9 Story-making in a global context

Figure 9.3 Students filming during a MECO presser in April 2016, photo courtesy of Maria Barbagallo

working as a journalist and producer with Channel NewsAsia, she is currently an independent journalist, host and moderator.

Peter Charley is another 2014 alumnus. Between 2011 and 2014, he studied part-time while working as executive producer of *Dateline* on SBS. Prior to that, he had been the executive producer of the ABC's *Lateline*. In late 2014, Al Jazeera approached him with an offer to take charge of their operations in North and South America. He tells us the MMP was "a highly valuable document" in their eyes. After seven years in Washington, DC, he is now based in Doha and manager of Al Jazeera's Investigative Unit. This means he is second in charge of the network's global investigative content, working under the director of the Investigative Directorate.

When we ask Charley how the MMP has contributed to his success, he tells us it "gave me fresh new perspectives on the media. Amongst other things, it helped me understand how the gathering and dissemination of information can be viewed through an academic lens – an entirely different take on the packaging of news and current affairs than I had experienced as a working reporter and producer."

In 2015, with Tim Dwyer as degree director and Fiona Giles as department chair, the credit point requirement jumped to 72. Students were now required to complete 24 credit points of core units, a maximum of 42 credit points of elective units and at least 6 credit points of capstone units. The 12-month full-time program that Shen, Ong and Charley completed became an 18-month program. Students were still learning media skills through the lenses of media theory and multidisciplinary knowledge, but the parameters of these skills and the depth of these lenses had increased.

The four core units remained the same and, from 2015, MECO electives were added covering financial and investor communication, health communication, social media communication, theoretical traditions and innovations, interviewing and research methods. Electives were also added from the Sydney College of the Arts, enabling MMP students to undertake units on sound design, photomedia and digital editing.

In the first year of the revamped degree, students could choose from three capstone units: MECO6904: Dissertation, MECO6928: Media and Communications Internship and MECO6935: Professional Practice. While the dissertation and internship had previously been electives, the professional practice unit was new. As Dwyer explains, formalising these units as capstones, and adding the third option, represented three complementary pathways for students. The dissertation offered a research track; the internship was focused on the workplace; and the professional track was "designed to enhance employment options for students through undertaking in-depth reports relevant to their own career interests".

Dwyer locates the tripling of MMP enrolments that occurred between 2017 and 2021 within a "uni-wide narrative" of increasing international student numbers. But the enhanced offerings following the degree restructure – and the steady honing since – have certainly played a part too. Dwyer names MECO6941, a podcasting elective introduced in 2018, as one example of the ongoing ways the degree is responding to "evolving media practices in platformised and social media app contexts".

Lea Redfern is behind MMP's evolution into podcasting. She tells us Megan Le Masurier proposed the idea for the elective and thinks it may have been the first postgraduate unit dedicated to podcasting at a university, in Australia or elsewhere. Redfern worked with independent podcaster Gretchen Miller to create the course content and has been coordinating the unit since its launch. In the first year, more than 100 students enrolled. Tina Matalov was the unit's original demonstrator, working alongside tutors in a role akin to an industry sound engineer. Redfern says she was "instrumental in creating a foundation of curiosity and fun within the course". Matalov now works at LiSTNR.

Olivia O'Flynn was one of Redfern's students in 2019. Since then, she has been nominated for three Australian Podcast Awards and, in 2021, was included in Radio Today's 30 Under 30 Awards. She is partner manager for the Creator

Figure 9.4 Students filming during a MECO presser in April 2016, photo courtesy of Maria Barbagallo

Network in Australia and New Zealand at Acast, which, she explains, involves "developing thought-leading formulas to drive podcast growth and understand audience behaviour". This year, O'Flynn was invited to sit on the judging panel for the Australian Podcast Awards. She credits MECO6941 with allowing her "to experiment and understand the medium of podcasting in a supported environment" and is grateful for the "lasting effect" of "Lea Redfern's pearls of wisdom and her generosity in sharing knowledge".

Enrolments in MECO6941 have increased each year, exceeding 500 in 2022. When we ask Redfern how she accounts for this popularity, she proposes a few reasons.

Foremost is that the unit "is taught almost exclusively by industry professionals who bring their rich experience and delight in audio to the classroom". Students also appreciate that it is a production unit, which means they are becoming familiar with new technology and gaining industry skills they can bring into the workforce. Their final assignment is to create a short podcast to broadcast standard, and they conclude the unit with "a real sense of achievement".

Students soon began asking for more, and in 2022 Redfern introduced MECO6947: Advanced Audio Project. This established another capstone option for MMP students, following on from the addition of MECO6932: Advanced Media Project (added in 2019) and MECO6946: Industry Research Project (added in 2021).

In the past few years, the degree has also added electives in publication design and managing social media communities. In 2019, the elective MECO6936: Social Media Communication replaced MECO6901: Dealing with the Media as one of the four core units. Bunty Avieson, who was degree director at the time, instigated the move as a response to the TEQSA review. The review noted the PR-oriented Dealing with the Media was in need of updating (it's since been renamed Media Relations and remains an elective) and saw an opportunity to add a core unit "addressing audiences and content creation and analytics across platforms, especially emerging digital ones".

The degree looks quite different than it did in 2004. The program and its units have evolved in response to a dynamic mediascape and ballooning enrolments. What remains at its core, though, in Avieson's words, is "telling stories about people. And those stories still have to be well told." Over the past two decades, more than 6,000 students have completed the degree. They have learned to create well-told stories about people across print, audio, video and multimedia modes, and they have learned to situate their story-making in professional, theoretical and global contexts. They have learned to put media into practice.

10
"I came because I could find no other degree like it": Digital Cultures

Cheryl O'Byrne

For five years, Miriam Landa worked for social media advertising agencies in Sydney. She developed campaign strategies, created content, managed influencers and reported on outcomes. It was, in her words, "boots on the ground" work. Landa outgrew the role, but not the industry. She began looking at postgraduate study options in the UK, the USA and Australia but wasn't finding anything suitable. Then Landa noticed the Master of Digital Communication and Culture at the University of Sydney. It was June 2020. She applied the same day and, within a week of receiving her acceptance letter, quit her job.

The program Landa arrived at has evolved from a Bachelor of Arts Informatics that began in 2000. Five years in, with insufficient enrolments, the Faculty of Arts and Social Sciences discontinued that degree. Kathy Cleland, Chris Chesher and John Tonkin reconstructed its units to form the basis of an undergraduate major and established a postgraduate program. These have proved prescient moves: in the first semester of 2021, eight percent of all FASS undergraduates are undertaking a Digital Cultures major or minor, which is astonishing given FASS undergraduates are choosing from more than 180 major/minor pathways. At the FASS postgraduate coursework level, there are more than 30 programs on offer, many of which include graduate certificate, graduate diploma and master's levels; once again, eight percent of these students are choosing Digital Cultures.

Many factors have contributed to this impressive rise, including increasing numbers of international students; the shift from undergraduate degree to major, which widened the pool of potential students; and the choice to join forces with MECO in 2013 (see Chapter 4). These are some of the details Chesher enumerated when I asked him about the program's success. Of the full-time faculty members who now teach and coordinate the program, Chesher is the one who's been there since the Arts Informatics days. "No one knew what Arts Informatics *was*" he told me; clearly the rebranding exercise was another wise move.

When I posed the same question to Marcus Carter, who joined the team in 2017, he offered a more literary response. He told me, "There is a fundamental diamond in this, something extremely valuable." As he said this, I could see, through my Zoom screen, that he was cupping his hands. What was he holding? To what does this metaphor refer? What are its contours, and what has pressed it into shape?

One of the defining forces has been the proliferation of digital media across the past two decades. As Chesher put it, his career "has paralleled the explosion in digital technology". Since he started at the University of Sydney in 2004, the field of digital media studies "has gone from a marginal speciality" to a discipline that "now everyone understands the importance of". When students explore the cultural context of "internet

10 "I came because I could find no other degree like it"

Figure 10.1 Marcus Carter, 2023, photo courtesy of the University of Sydney

platforms, social media, research tools, digital audiences, mobile media, online governance, cross-media creative and games", as the postgraduate program description promises, they are noticing anew the water through which they swim.

One postgraduate student, Nicole Lewis, who is 23, told me, "I've grown up with this [technology], but now is the first time I'm thinking critically about its impact." Other students I spoke to made similar observations. When Vaibhavi Deshpande arrived, she was looking for a framework to understand the role of social media algorithms in her children's lives. Lan Yang told me a highlight for her has been reconsidering video games through the lens of feminist theory in ARIN6904: Games and Mixed Realities. Carter, who coordinates that unit, thinks it's this kind of curiosity that characterises the cohort: the students want to understand the relationship between these omnipresent digital platforms and the culture that both shapes and is shaped by them.

For most students, the curiosity that drove them to the Digital Cultures program is founded in their personal relationship to digital media. For others, like Landa, the relationship also has been professional; their experiences working within digital industries have engendered a desire to enlarge their perspectives and career prospects. Lewis's internship at a communications firm in Miami prompted her interest in postgraduate study.

Another student, Tony Perna, is the assistant director of a campaign design and social media team for an Australian government agency. He told me that he's learned most of what he knows about digital media from colleagues, and now the Digital Cultures program is providing an invaluable theoretical perspective. As someone who leads a team of employees, he wants to learn "to step away and understand what we do, to have a bigger picture". "Why entrust this to the team at Sydney?" I asked. His response: "There is no other degree quite like it."

I asked seven students to help me put together this story, all of whom I met while I was teaching ARIN6903: Digital Media and Society last semester under Chesher's leadership.

10 "I came because I could find no other degree like it"

Perna's response became a refrain that sounded through each of those conversations: I came because I could find no other degree quite like it. This is Landa's story. It is also Lewis's, who searched for a USA-based option but found that the University of Sydney "was exactly what I was after". It is also Yang's story, who transferred after undergraduate media studies at the University of Melbourne; Yulan Wu's, who transferred from media at UNSW; and Hanlin Wang's, who came after completing undergraduate media studies at a university in China.

The unique combination of digital studies and cultural studies is also what has attracted academics to the program. Justine Humphry began teaching at the University of Sydney in 2011, after completing a PhD on the way smartphones were transforming work practices and instituting a culture of mobility and flexibility. She taught into the undergraduate major and the master's degree, developing and shaping a number of courses and the direction of the program. After four years of fixed-term contracts and a research fellowship, she moved to Western Sydney University, where she created a new unit on digital cultures. When an opportunity arose to return to the University of Sydney in early 2017, Humphry jumped at the chance. She was drawn back because of the program's "very pioneering work, centring digital and social change as the core focus of the teaching and research". Humphry said, "It was the only academic environment I'd come across where that was the focus and not an add-on." She named some similar programs now available in Australia (at institutions like Curtin University, Queensland University of Technology, RMIT University and Monash University) but emphasised "ours is unique" and, "in 2017, we were the only ones doing that kind of work".

Figure 10.2 Justine Humphry, 2017, photo courtesy of the University of Sydney

Olga Boichak came to Sydney in October 2019 after finishing her PhD at Syracuse University and likens the experience of meeting her new colleagues to "finding a family". After years researching digital media within the Syracuse social science department, the Digital Cultures program, she said, "gave me an identity that I didn't have before". Mark Johnson told a similar story: he also joined the Digital Cultures team in October 2019, after postdocs in sociology, computer science and political science departments in London and Alberta. Like Boichak, the Sydney team afforded him the opportunity to situate his work among other digital media scholars. The

10 "I came because I could find no other degree like it"

Figure 10.3 Olga Boichak, 2023, photo by Stefanie Zingsheim

program, it seems, has become a home for likeminded trailblazers.

Their convergence has been so successful, in part, because of the way they are pursuing a common purpose while still retaining distinctive research agendas. A conversation is occurring between Boichak's work on digital activism and digital war; Johnson's on live streaming and gamification; Humphry's on the social consequences of mobile, smart and data-driven technologies; Carter's on virtual reality and

Figure 10.4 Mark Johnson, 2021, photo by Mark Johnson

augmented reality; and Chesher's on robotics, urban informatics and invocational media. As Carter described it, there is no "top down" approach operating; when new scholars joined the team, they were not asked to acquiesce to any "clear vision" of what the program does or where the limits of the digital cultures field lie. Instead, they've been asked to help contemplate these fundamental, shifting questions.

This collaborative approach occurs in various forums, including the monthly Digital Cultures Research Cluster meetings wherein team members and guests present and invite discussion about their latest research. Such work was promoted by the Socio-Technical Futures (STuF) Lab, established in 2018, and is being advanced through the new Centre for Digital Technologies and Societies, established in 2023. Collaboration is also happening when colleagues work together on international research teams, such as the investigation of street-smart furniture with scholars in Scotland or the investigation of robots in public space with colleagues in Korea. The aim, Humphry told me, has been to create "an environment that is inclusive and encouraging, shaping both the program and the field".

The give-and-take ethos that characterises the team is also evident in their approach to teaching. In 2021, the team launched two new units, both of which had been developed cooperatively and are taught cooperatively. Whereas first-year Digital Cultures majors used to complete MECO1001 and MECO1002, which were shared with the Media and Communications students, they now undertook ARIN1001: The Past and Futures of Digital Cultures. Humphry, as Digital Cultures major coordinator, had led this development process, involving Digital Cultures colleagues in the design and inviting each to deliver a guest lecture in their area of speciality. Likewise, Carter, as postgraduate coordinator, launched ARIN6909: Emerging Technologies and Issues, a new core unit that all five scholars helped design and help teach.

As I spoke with Chesher, Humphry, Carter, Boichak and Johnson between December 2020 and February 2021, in the wake of a pandemic year, I heard them speak of one another with admiration and deep gratitude. I also began to recognise that the qualities they seemed to value most in their team were the qualities they sought to nurture in their virtual classrooms. Boichak, for example, told me how she tries to "adopt a philosophy of conviviality" where "students are learning through each other, getting to know each other and working together". As part of this, she looks for ways "to create a sense of accomplishment, to celebrate achievement and to foster connections". Johnson expressed his appreciation for the increase in one-on-one interactions with students that the online environment enabled. Carter, too, said one of his greatest achievements over the previous, fraught year was the way he was able to maintain connections with Digital Cultures PhD students over virtual coffees, a reading group and a network that they opened to PhD students internationally.

Perhaps we can say, then, that the "fundamental diamond" around which this program turns has been formed because of institutional decision-making and the cultural context of proliferating digital media. We can also say it has been extracted, and is being buffed to a shine, by the scholars who have been tasked with protecting it. Like all good metaphors, this one, in Carter's words, "resists defining", and that's also part of its charm. When studying a field that is expanding daily, and with a group of scholars who offer distinct perspectives on that field, any attempt to define its parameters would necessarily diminish it. We can say, though, that Digital Cultures at Sydney is a site of unique interdisciplinary inquiry; of respectful, open-minded collaboration; and of expert-led education.

A comment Johnson made prompts me to add the "expert-led" modifier. He's noticed that "there is no space and no field of work that attracts more charlatans than digital media". When we've all become users of digital media and we're all online with "some degree of competence" we might start to think we are experts. On the contrary, Johnson maintains, the current moment "makes *genuine* expertise important to foreground".

Terry Flew, as genuine an expert as one could imagine, became the sixth full-time member of the team in April 2021. As I was finishing this chapter, I asked him what he envisages for the future of teaching within the field. One element that must be high on our agenda, he insists, is *power*. Most students come to us with a high level of technical proficiency, but what we offer them is a holistic and demystifying view. In our post-digital environment, where effectively all media is digital media, and media power is concentrated in the hands of a small number of technology companies, it is increasingly important, he contends, that our students engage with this concentration of power in terms of ethics, law and policy.

Some of our graduates will work for these digital behemoths and may, as Flew points out, join the trend whereby employees are becoming vocal critics. Other students have different plans. Landa wants to be part of governmental policy-making conversations and has her eye on the department of the Australian eSafety Commissioner. Lewis wants to work for a humanitarian organisation and oversee the creation of digital campaign materials that can reach people, like her, "who want to see the art of it all".

11
Between theory and practice: teaching public relations
Cheryl O'Byrne and Sylvie Chen

There is a photograph on Mitchell Hobbs's bookshelf that was taken at a Christmas party on the back lawn of The Lodge in 2011. He is standing beside Prime Minister Julia Gillard. Both are looking at the camera, smiling warmly and have an arm behind the other's back. At the time, Hobbs was working for the prime minister as a media and electorate stakeholder officer. He had begun the role shortly after completing his PhD on the politics of Rupert Murdoch's News Corporation, in 2010, and delighted in the way it enabled him to apply his academic research to this real-world context.

A few months after posing for this photo, however, a choice to support his partner's career, in Sydney, meant he was leaving the job behind. Hobbs speaks candidly about the regret he felt at the time. But he also saw it as an opportunity to return to academia, teach and pursue the questions that had been accumulating since he finished the PhD. So, in 2015, he began a new position: lecturer and degree director for the Master of Strategic Public Relations (MSPR) at the University of Sydney. Inspired by his experience on Gillard's staff, he

Figure 11.1 Mitchell Hobbs, 2023, photo by Gunther Hang

set out determined that the degree would balance the highest calibre of theoretical inquiry with the attainment of practical, industry-based skills.

Richard Stanton launched the MSPR in 2006 and led the program for its first eight years. Sean Chaidaroon worked with him for some of this time. Then Alana Mann oversaw the

11 Between theory and practice

degree before handing the reins to Hobbs. The four core units that Stanton established have remained central to the degree: MECO6908: Strategy Selection in Corporate PR, MECO6909: PR Management and Conflict Resolution (renamed Crisis Communication in 2016), MECO6912: Political Public Relations and MECO6913: Public Opinion, Policy and Public Sphere. The degree structure continues to resemble Stanton's original vision, but the units themselves have been transformed. Two years ago, Hobbs received a Dean's Award for Excellence in Teaching, which acknowledged his innovative redevelopment of the PR curriculum.

Hobbs explains that MSPR units need to instil "critical understanding of [the PR practitioner's] place in the world and significance, and the ethics and responsibilities that come with their skills". At the same time, "students also need to know how to apply those skills, how to localise that knowledge, and how to put that into action in a way that can generate results". Interweaving these two pedagogical concerns – the understanding and the application – has been part of the degree since its inception, but Hobbs has made this a key priority. Their confluence ensures that graduates "can basically hit the ground running in their employment".

Part of Hobbs's redesign involved mapping this vision onto the units' assessment tasks. He explains, "We created a mix-model of assessment. Many of the assessments are now focused on the attainment of industry skills by requiring students to develop a portfolio of professional work. Other assessments seek to foster scholastic outcomes and critical reflexivity regarding the practice of public relations."

Hobbs and his team ensure the *"understanding"* component of the curriculum covers the various paradigms that comprise the field of public relations – from systems and ecology theories to dialogue, rhetoric and the critical school. "Previously the program had a strong focus on systems and public sphere approaches, which are still relevant and something that I use in my own research, but there are other perspectives out there, which are more dominant in North America and Europe," Hobbs says. "So, I make it a point to attend the PR Division of the ICA [International Communications Association] Conference as regularly as possible, in order to bring the latest scholarship back to our program at Sydney." Students consider public relations through a range of theoretical lenses: ethical, legal, political, cultural and social.

The "*application*" component finds students developing a range of professional outputs for creative agencies using integrative communications. Students prepare campaign portfolios that incorporate various tactics, including writing media releases, organising events, writing speeches, planning budgets, harnessing social media and using industry-standard software for designing flyers and brochures. Students are applying quantitative and qualitative research methods and deploying strategies to evaluate the effectiveness of their campaigns.

Hobbs also encourages MSPR graduates to develop necessary soft skills, such as level-headedness. "There's so much vitriol on social media and so many trolls. Companies and organisations will face all sorts of criticism as part of their daily operations, and good PR people need to leave their emotions at the door, not take things personally, and engage with genuine criticism and feedback," he says. Hobbs knows that the ability to remain calm in a conflict scenario or crisis is an essential quality. He teaches students to foresee a PR situation and ask, "What do I need to protect? What do I need to change? What do I need to advocate for?" Their responses must align with an ethical practice that is "transparent, respectful of the audience [and] seeking to have win-win outcomes for organisations and stakeholders."

In addition, Hobbs and his team prioritise written and interpersonal communication. "The ability to work with people, journalists, colleagues, and to be enthusiastic and engaging – being enthusiastic about your job and having other people catch that enthusiasm – is such an important skill in PR, which is all about relationships," Hobbs says.

He dwells on the working-with-journalists part. Hobbs worries that "public relations somewhat unfairly has a reputation problem" and suspects this is "because there's a bit of a professional misunderstanding between journalists and PR practitioners." He describes their relationship as marked by the "occasional power struggle". Studies show that 60 to 70 percent of mass media content comes from PR work, yet it is "the journalists and editors and producers who decide what goes into the media cycle". PR practitioners need to navigate some tricky terrain to ensure this "symbiotic" relationship is functional. This is one reason why, in 2019, Hobbs changed the name of the popular elective MECO6901 from the adversarial Dealing with the Media to the more diplomatic Media Relations.

In October 2017, after a thorough application process, the Public Relations Institute of Australia (PRIA) accredited the MSPR. PRIA endorses degrees that "ensure their courses align with current industry practice", employ staff who "play a vital role in progressing the profession in concert with the industry body" and equip their graduates "with best practice skills and competencies". In other words, this achievement affirmed how successfully the MSPR (alongside its Graduate

Certificate and Graduate Diploma pathways) has managed to bridge the divide between academic knowledge creation and industry. Currently, the University of Sydney is one of only two institutions in New South Wales that can claim this distinction at the postgraduate level, and one of only six in Australia.

Hobbs is quick to ascribe the PR program's success to the commitment and expertise of his teaching team. Until February 2022, when Catherine Page Jeffery was appointed as a second full-time staff member, Hobbs was the only full-time, ongoing PR staff member. But he has surrounded himself with a casual teaching team made up of industry leaders. Sally Tindall, who was Gillard's senior press secretary, teaches MECO6912: Political PR. She and others – such as Matthew Abbott (former Head of Communications at ASIC and now director of corporate affairs at *Zip Co*), Michelle Innis (former journalist for *The New York Times* and now senior consultant at P&L Corporate Communications) and Julia Booth (a communications consultant and author) – have been helping to create an academic culture that produces industry-ready graduates. Their students are finding employment in PR fields such as public and corporate affairs, government communication, and financial and investor communication.

Those graduates are a measure of the program's effectiveness – and a source of pride. "All my students seem to get jobs and they do quite well in industry," Hobbs says. "Several of my students have gone on to start in an industry, climbed the corporate ladder and now are coming back and doing casual teaching with the department." This includes Paul Allen, who is a Bloomberg Australian TV anchor, and Jessie Nguyen, who is an account manager at Primary

11 Between theory and practice

Communication and a councillor for the City of Canterbury Bankstown.

Another is Charlotte Launder, who completed the MSPR in 2015. When asked to name what was most formative, she recalls assessments that enabled her to design and implement a media relations campaign for a not-for-profit restaurant, develop PR strategies for a local surf lifesaving club, and take part in a political campaign. These experiences gave her "exposure to the industry and the opportunity to apply the skills [she] was learning in class". Since graduating, Launder has worked at global and boutique PR agencies. Her career took her to London where she specialised in travel and tourism PR. "Being able to travel around Europe while representing industry-leading airlines, hotel groups, cruise lines and destinations has been a highlight of my career to date," she says.

Since 2019, Launder has been combining freelance PR work with teaching. Her initial responsibility was to MECO2603: Public Relations. This undergraduate unit has been part of the Bachelor of Arts (MECO) curriculum since Catharine Lumby introduced the degree – the only strategic communications unit in a degree otherwise focused on media communications. The unit falls under Hobbs's purview as MSPR degree director and was part of the redevelopment process he initiated when he assumed that role. One of his first moves was to change the name of the unit, and its scope, from Media Relations – which is just one component of PR – to Public Relations. He describes MECO2603 as a "very sharp" unit that compresses all the best content from across the MSPR units. Introducing media undergrads to PR serves both to broaden their career horizons and help breakdown those "hostilities and professional rivalries" that can plague the journalist–PR practitioner dynamic.

Hobbs names Clare Davies as another accomplished alumna who has returned to teach MSPR students. She graduated with a Master of Health Communication (MHC, see Chapter 13) and her affiliation with MSPR illustrates the close relationship between these two MECO degrees. (Indeed, the two degrees share Crisis Communication as a core unit, which MHC degree director Olaf Werder coordinates.) Davies teaches across MSPR and MHC units. As she explains, "The relationship between PR and HC has always been important, but its role in communicating accurate and trustworthy information that improves individual lives has become critical over the last few years." Coupled with the evolving media and digital landscape, "Practitioners need to look at novel ways to translate complex issues into communications strategies that empower audiences to take action for their health."

Practitioners in this field borrow skills inherent to PR: building relationships, facilitating two-way dialogue and innovating communication methods. Davies's current position epitomises this intersection: she is a PR professional who specialises in the health and pharmaceutical industries. She is a senior account director at WE Communications and across her career has worked with AstraZeneca, Johnson & Johnson, Pfizer, Roche, the Department of Health and the National Breast Cancer Foundation. Davies's PhD project, examining the factors that create, support and reproduce normative ideals of individual health and female embodiment, also stretches across the PR and HC fields.

It is easy to see why MECO colleagues, alumni, industry leaders and contacts from Gillard's circle have been quick to support Hobbs's ambitions for the program. These ambitions

11 Between theory and practice

originated in a conversation that occurred during the earliest days of his work with Gillard. In a Melbourne office, Hobbs was explaining Foucault's theory of discursive power to another Gillard media advisor. A few minutes in, the advisor responded, "That's really interesting. But what can you actually *do* with it?"

"Ever since then," Hobbs says, "I've always been focused on [asking] *how is this applied? How can this knowledge be used to have some actual, tangible outcome?*" When Hobbs shares this anecdote, he is referring to his own research. But it's clear that this "penny drop" moment has shaped the MSPR program too. Throughout their degree, MSPR students are learning both to theorise and to do. For Hobbs, as academic, practitioner, degree director and teacher, "that was a really good lesson."

12
"A community of practice and professional discourse": the Master of Publishing

Agata Mrva-Montoya

In November 2007, Amazon released the Kindle in the USA. While not the first ereader on the market, this quaint looking gadget, with its small vertical screen above rows of round buttons, disrupted the global publishing industry. An industry already threatened by the rise of self-publishing and beset by blockbuster mergers and acquisitions was now facing a growing imperative to release books in digital formats. It was within this dynamic environment that the first intake of students joined the Master of Publishing at the University of Sydney.

Fiona Giles, the driving force behind the establishment of the degree, told me that the Master of Publishing was set up to fill an obvious gap in postgraduate coursework offerings by universities in New South Wales. She said, "At the time, in 2007, there were only two postgraduate coursework alternatives in the Sydney region, and neither were full master's programs." The University of Technology Sydney had a Graduate Certificate in Editing and Publishing, offered since 2002, while Macquarie University had a Graduate Diploma in Editing and Publishing, offered since 1989. Outside the university context, Macleay College began offering a Diploma in Book Editing and Publishing in 1988 (but the degree was stopped in 2017).

The Master of Publishing at the University of Sydney aimed to cover three areas of the publishing industry in depth: books, magazines and online publishing. Giles said, "The online component at the time was also supported by the Master of Digital Cultures, which Chris Chesher was developing in parallel with the Master of Publishing, so for a few years we shared some of our units. This made our degree distinctive from the other degrees and resulted in broader options for graduates when seeking work following their studies. As online publishing became even more important the balance changed slightly, but the idea was still to be comprehensive in this way."

Traditionally, publishing skills were acquired on the job as an apprenticeship. Individuals, usually with an Arts degree, would start as editorial assistants and work their way up to become editors and publishers. Professional development and in-service courses first appeared in the 1950s in the USA, while the first university-based degrees were established in the early 1960s in the UK. In the global context, as John Maxwell writes in his 2014 article, "publishing education arose in the 20th century in response to a need for trained employees in a stable industry with a well understood set of competencies and skills".[1] These requirements changed at the beginning of the 21st century, as a result of the digital disruption and acceleration of technical developments affecting the industry. Since then, the publishing degrees have operated in a constant

---

1   Maxwell, 2014.

state of flux as new skills are required from graduates. This has certainly been the case with the Master of Publishing at the University of Sydney, which has continued evolving at the level of individual units and the whole curriculum.

The degree started with four core units: MECO6914: Making Magazines, MECO6916: Editing and Manuscript Preparation, MECO6917: Book Production and Publishing Business and ARIN6912: Digital Research and Publishing. In addition to these units, students could select electives from across postgraduate units offered by MECO, English and other departments in the Faculty of Arts and Social Sciences.

Since the beginning, with the exception of MECO6914 taught by Megan Le Masurier until 2012, the degree has relied on sessional staff for teaching, while being overseen by the degree director. Giles mentioned staffing as the ongoing challenge through the life of the degree. She said, "We've had amazing lecturers from the publishing industry who have taught for several years, before other commitments no longer made this possible. It's just a shame we haven't had the resources to offer any of these highly qualified individuals a continuing position."

The key industry professionals who have contributed their expertise and knowledge and taught generations of students include Gregor Stronach, Andrea Duvall, Leigh Reinhold, Sam Cooney, Lucy Cousins and Matt Coyte (MECO6914); Nicola O'Shea, Deonie Fiford, Roberta Ivers, Louise Thurtell, Richard Walsh, Craig Munro, Joanne Butler, Rochelle Fernandez and Claire Linsdell (MECO6916); and Rowanne Couch, Anna Maguire and Franscois McHardy (MECO6917). Maguire said, "Staying across industry trends and with a deep knowledge of how the publishing industry works, gave me an understanding of what knowledge and skills new entrants would require and enabled me to give students a holistic understanding of the business of publishing." Apart from sessional staff, many other professionals have shared their expertise as guest lecturers. Being taught by industry specialists has been crucial for the success of the degree. As Maguire said, "Many things work well in theory, but first-hand knowledge is key."

Over time, gaps in the curriculum became evident and more units were added. The importance of learning basic industry software such as Adobe InDesign for book and magazine publishing led to the introduction of MECO6930: Publication Design in 2011. Initially, Megan Le Masurier and Fiona Giles collaborated with a freelance designer, then with the Sydney College of the Arts, which was running a similar unit. Eventually, MECO6930 became completely housed within MECO and replaced ARIN6912 in the list of core units for the Master of Publishing. The unit has been a huge success and remains popular beyond the publishing degree, with Digital Media and other students keen to learn the theory and practice of graphic design. It has been taught by many talented graphic designers including Katherine Sorrenson, Julieta Ormeno, Sharon Metzl, Fleur Anson, David Corbert, Sonia Blaskovic, Gary Humphries, Robin Austin, Matt Caulfield, Sharon Brown and Amanda LeMay.

When I joined the teaching team as a sessional lecturer in 2016, I developed a new unit, MECO6937: Making eBooks and Digital Magazines, using my research into multimedia publishing and my experience in the production of ebooks at Sydney University Press as the starting point.[2] The unit's double focus on digital skills relevant for both magazine and book publishing industries resulted in ongoing contradictory

---

2 Mrva-Montoya, 2015.

12 "A community of practice and professional discourse"

Figure 12.1 Agata Mrva-Montoya, 2016, photo courtesy of the University of Sydney

feedback from students who, depending where they saw their future careers, preferred a focus on one or the other. This was symptomatic of the degree as a whole. As Le Masurier said, "we were trying to cram too much into too few units". Moreover, it became apparent that the majority of students were interested in book publishing.

Anna Maguire and I spent many hours at the Taste Café in the New Law Building brainstorming how to meet the demand for more units focusing on book publishing and how to update the degree in response to the industry's needs. The publishing industry had evolved dramatically since 2007. According to a 2016 report on the disruption and innovation in the Australian book industry, "Major changes include the development of technology which enables digital publishing, distribution and retailing; the entry of disruptive players including Amazon, Google and Apple; the introduction of handheld digital reading platforms and devices; upheavals in the bricks and mortar retailing sector; and the rise of online and social media as important channels for promoting books."[3] Moreover, ebooks were continuing to rise in popularity, and the production of audiobooks was also on the rise. The legal context had also changed. Following the implementation of the Marrakesh Treaty to Facilitate Access to Published Works for Persons Who Are Blind, Visually Impaired or Otherwise Print Disabled in Australia in 2016, the Australian Inclusive Publishing Initiative was established to facilitate the industry's move towards the production of "born-accessible" content. Accessibility and metadata became household terms.

In February 2018, after several long lunches, we came up with a proposal to review three of the existing units and create two new ones. We consulted broadly with industry professionals who provided feedback on the proposed outlines and learning objectives of the five units. The results of an industry skills survey run by the Australian Publishers Association in 2018 confirmed that the restructure of the degree was heading in the right direction.

---

3   Zwar, 2016, p. i.

Le Masurier supported, shaped and shepherded the proposal through the university approval system. The new version of the degree had two streams, one focusing on book publishing and the other on magazine publishing. MECO6916: Editing and Proofreading and MECO6930: Publication Design remained core for both pathways. Students interested in book publishing would go on to study MECO6917: Book Publishing Business and MECO6937: Book Design and Production (later renamed Producing Books in the Digital Age), and they had two new electives to choose from: MECO6943: Book Sales and Marketing (taught first by Maguire and then Rachael McDiarmid) and MECO6944: Manuscript Acquisition and Development (taught first by Rodney Morrison, then Bernadette Foley and Linda Funnell). Students wanting to enter the magazine publishing industry were required to study MECO6914: Making Magazines and ENGL6970: Reading Magazines and were able to select from journalism-focused electives such as MECO6915: Writing Feature Stories.

Students in both streams could also select a new unit on podcasting. As Le Masurier said, "It became clear to me that our publishing students needed to be skilled in multimedia. Four years ago, podcasting was clearly on the rise, and it was being used amongst all kinds of media organisations, including books and magazines." Lea Redfern, who first started teaching podcasting at the undergraduate level, wrote and taught the first postgraduate podcasting course, MECO6941, in Semester 2, 2018. This unit has since become a highly popular elective for postgraduate students from the MECO master's degrees.

Apart from the ongoing development of the curriculum, other key milestones included getting the degree accredited with the Australian Publisher Association in 2010, and the establishment of a separate degree director for each of the postgraduate degrees from 2013 onwards. As Le Masurier said, "Until then, Fiona Giles had administered all the master's degrees. This separation of roles allowed for far more focused attention to be placed on each degree." Le Masurier remained the degree director until 2020, when I took over the role.

The year 2020 turned out to be entirely different from what anyone expected. Following the discovery of the first case of COVID-19 on campus (see Chapter 19), we moved all teaching online in one week in the middle of March, along with the rest of the University. It was a tough year for both staff and students, but at the same time it was an amazing learning experience as we spent much time on Zoom looking into each other's private spaces, collaborating online and making the technology work for us. So did the publishing industry around the world, with the move to working from home and the need to rely exclusively on marketing and launching books digitally. The importance of digital skills had never been more obvious.

The students of Publishing tend to come with a BA in English, communication or linguistics, though we also have had individuals with undergraduate degrees in acting, archaeology, creative writing, history, law and other disciplines. They are all united by the love of books and reading. The majority want to become editors and publishers of the next *Harry Potter*. Some want to be writers and undertake the degree to expand their understanding of the industry, or perhaps self-publish in the future. The ratio of students interested in magazine publishing has dropped over the years, reflecting the changing fortunes of the magazine industry in Australia.

One of the missions of the degree is to open students' eyes to the variety of job opportunities across all sectors of the industry. Apart from the highly coveted trade book publishing, interesting and rewarding roles can be found in educational and professional book publishing, and of course working with authors wanting to self-publish. In Australia, the world of magazines has been beset by mergers and the loss of jobs. Despite this, new opportunities are emerging for niche content, targeting more selective audiences. As Le Masurier said, "There's actually the secret side to the magazine industry: the business-to-business, customer magazines and indie publications have been flourishing."

In its current iteration, the degree provides students with core publishing skills and knowledge across the various aspects of publishing: commissioning and acquisition; editorial; design for print, digital and audio delivery; print production; budgeting and finance; and sales and marketing. While students may aspire to and end up working in a specific role, the degree gives them an understanding of the whole publishing workflow so that they are well prepared to work constructively with authors and other professionals in these inherently collaborative industries. To that effect, several of the units have a group work component to enable students to develop the all-important skills of collaborating and managing projects.

The internship has been a core element of the degree since the beginning. It allows students to apply and advance their knowledge and skills in an organisational setting, develop their professional identity, and foster professional networks prior to graduation. In 2018, we introduced a diagnostic test for students to take before they can apply for an internship, to make sure they are "job ready" for their time at a host organisation. As part of the unit, they write an industry report exploring a current challenge and its impact on graduate employability, and a reflection on the process of integrating degree and workplace learning during the internship. Over the years, MECO has developed close collaborations with a number of magazine and book publishers and other organisations who host our students, including Allen & Unwin, the Australian Publishers Association, Curtis Brown, Echo Publishing, Halstead Press, Pan Macmillan, Pantera Press, Sydney University Press, Spineless Wonders, *Vogue Australia*, *Fashion Journal* and many other publishers and publications. Our interns are highly regarded.

They are also highly regarded graduates. Our alumni have had jobs at Allen and Unwin, Murdoch Books, NewSouth Books, Pantera Press, Penguin Random House, Scholastic, Simon and Schuster, Sydney University Press, Walker Books, the Australian Publishers Association and the National Museum of Australia. Overseas, our graduates have worked for Bloomsbury and the Natural History Museum in London; Ediciones Uniandes, Universidad de los Andes in Bogota, Columbia; and Bonnier and Star Stable Entertainment in Sweden. In the magazine industry, we have had alumni working for NewsLifeMedia, *The CEO Magazine*, and many others.

Giving students the opportunity to get practical experience has also underpinned the University of Sydney Student Anthology project. The year-long student-led project has been running since the degree began in 2007. When Fiona Giles was developing the program, she consulted widely with industry professionals, writers and academics. Two people in particular inspired the idea: Drusilla Modjeska (then an honorary associate in the English department at the University of Sydney) and Catherine Cole (from the University of Technology Sydney program). Giles recalled, "I also consulted with Sydney University Press who were happy to publish the anthology and Gleebooks who were happy to assist with the launch and marketing." The rationale was to provide students with a real-world publishing experience, within a committee formed each year as an extra-curricular activity. The project was managed by a casual lecturer – first Keith Stevenson, then Mark Rossiter, and later Gregor Stronach.

In 2016, I took over the coordination of the project. My association with the anthology goes a long way back. I was a student member of the anthology team in 2008 and have remained involved in some way in the final stages of production in every anthology since then on behalf of Sydney University Press. Remembering the difficulties in coming up with the title for a thematically disparate collection of works, the first thing I did was introduce an annual theme to the anthology. Phil Glen and Marc Fernando from the Digital Media Unit built a new website for us, which streamlined the submission process and provided a showcase for the collection.

While the anthology project has evolved over the years, the key objectives have remained the same. The students solicit work from the university student cohort in Semester 1. At the beginning of Semester 2, the fate of each work is decided during a long submission meeting. Then the editorial and design processes start. Each anthology features a foreword written by a renowned literary figure, with past contributors including Larissa Behrendt, Shankari Chandran, Ceridwen Dovey, Kate Forsyth, Maeve Marsden, PM Newton, Diane Reid and Mark Tredinnick. Since 2015, the launch has been combined with a welcome to the new publishing students and a call for new team members in Week 2 of Semester 1.

The project has typically attracted between ten and 25 student volunteers each year. Apart from the website,

Figure 12.2 Cover of *Earth cries* (2021), designed by Emily Bronte Smith and Mary Stanley

www.usydanthology.com, the anthology has a Facebook page, and Instagram and Twitter/X accounts. Being part of the anthology team is a lot of work but as Chelsea Sutherland, who participated in 2017 and 2018 said,

> It's a great learning experience, whatever field of publishing you're interested in working in. It provides

a fantastic opportunity to be actively involved in the entire publication process, from developing a theme to launching a finished book. The project offers hands-on experience in editorial, marketing, design and production, and gives you a chance to apply and hone the skills you've learned in class, and to step out of your comfort zone and develop new skills. The anthology gave me the opportunity to learn to design and typeset a book and piqued my interest in production, a career path I'd never really considered. It's also a great chance to meet and work with other students and staff in the Master of Publishing and across the University.

Following the horrific fires in the summer of 2019–20, students decided to focus the 2020 anthology on climate change. And then the pandemic hit, which meant we had to move our meetings and all marketing online. The university campus was empty so there was no point putting up posters, not even on the usually busy Eastern Avenue or at Fisher Library. With no posters and the impact of COVID-19, we struggled to get submissions. A new strategy was required. We opened the call for new works to all University of Sydney staff, alumni and students, and we ended up with a strong collection, with a foreword by Karl Kruszelnicki.

Le Masurier and Giles also tried to set up a project for magazine students alongside the anthology, but this was stymied by the University's marketing policy. Giles said, "It would still make a wonderful project – if the resources were available – and enable the students to showcase not only their writing and editing but their design skills."

Over the years, we have also tried to set up a student-led publishing house to build on the success of the anthology, and to further combine project-based, on-the-job learning with mentoring and interdisciplinary teaching. Such teaching and student-led publishing houses are associated with many publishing degrees in Australia (at RMIT, the University of Melbourne and the University of Queensland) and internationally. With the limited resources available in the University post-COVID-19, this idea has been placed on hold.

So, what about the future of the Master of Publishing? Fifteen years later, it remains the only master's level publishing degree in New South Wales. Le Masurier said, "The degree will constantly be updated as the industry continues to change. In the immediate future, I see the focus being more on book publishing than magazine publishing. The magazine unit will still run, but as an elective open to other MECO degrees (such as Master of Media Practice) rather than a core for MPub." She also said she believed a new multimedia unit needed to be developed at the master's level, where students can learn basic video shooting, editing and voiceover narrative skills.

Apart from the evolving curriculum, Giles said when I talked to her in 2020, "The degree would have a stronger and more secure future if MECO could appoint at least one permanent continuing lecturer." Such an appointment would complement the industry expertise of the sessional lectures, providing a more solid research base to the curriculum design, teaching delivery and, most importantly, student learning. This came to pass in January 2022, when I joined MECO on a full-time basis. According to Giles, the degree "has had consistently strong enrolments in the vicinity of 40 to 50 students per semester, with some of the units enrolling many more". She said, "The size, while not of blockbuster scale such as some of the other MECO programs, is not only economically viable but good for the students, who can get to know each other as a cohort, work together on the anthology and develop their networking skills with the industry-based staff and their internship experience. Given that the publishing industry is itself relatively small in Australia, the student numbers have been admirable."

According to John Maxwell, director of Publishing at Simon Fraser University, these days publishing degrees need to deliver more than just teaching specific skills. They need to provide "an environment that nurtures a community of practice and professional discourse in which to develop [students'] already-existing sensibilities ... they enter into this environment collectively and together undergo the process of learning and becoming valuable professionals. They are working individually and collectively: acquiring and generating knowledge, and perspectives, and the very culture of publishing."[4]

By constantly evolving, experimenting and working closely together with the industry, the Master of Publishing is well placed to provide forward-looking professional training and contribute to the publishing culture of Australia. While the long-term impacts of the pandemic are hard to predict, it is clear that it has accelerated the digitisation trends across various aspects of the publishing industry, including ebook consumption, and forced publishers to be more creative and collaborative. The publishers also need to become more inclusive in their hiring and publishing strategies to better represent and cater for the voices of First Nations and People of Colour, and people with disabilities. Curious, innovative

---

4   Maxwell, 2014.

and resilient graduates are what the industry needs and what the Master of Publishing at the University of Sydney is producing.

Works cited

Maxwell, J.W. (2014). Publishing education in the 21st century and the role of the university. *Journal of Electronic Publishing, 17*(2). https://doi.org/10.3998/3336451.0017.205

Mrva-Montoya, A. (2015). Beyond the monograph: publishing research for multimedia and multiplatform delivery. *Journal of Scholarly Publishing, 46*(4), 321–42. http://dx.doi.org/10.3138/jsp.46.4.02

Zwar, J. (2016). *Disruption and innovation in the Australian book industry: Case studies of trade and education publishers.* Macquarie Economics Research Papers, Department of Economics, Macquarie University. https://apo.org.au/node/68152

13
Crossing disciplines to improve lives: the Master of Health Communication

Olaf Werder

The health communication program, introduced at the University of Sydney in Semester 1, 2009, was the brainchild of two academics, Simon Chapman from the School of Public Health and Fiona Giles of MECO. It came about to fill a void in the public health teaching program, namely mediated discourse, journalistic activity and promotions in public health. Over the years, the program has moved away from this focused orientation to include broader perspectives on the health communication process. It continues to combine the expertise of MECO, where all the core courses are located, with the resources of the School of Public Health, where students can choose from a plethora of elective courses. Subsequently, this cross-disciplinary and collaborative approach to both media and health disciplines has made the program the most comprehensive and specialised course of its kind in Australia.

I have directed the program since I arrived at the University in 2011. I hold a senior lectureship in strategic and health communication, after having held similar positions at the University of Florida and the University of New Mexico.

Figure 13.1 Olaf Werder, 2018, photo courtesy of the University of Sydney

Prior to my academic appointments, I worked in the communication industry on the media and agency side in two countries for about 10 years. Health communication is a crucial function for public health. I am trying to teach people to understand what communication does and can do, and how it can be improved. Coincidentally, in the new normal of living in a pandemic, health has become a very relevant concern, where students more readily see the relationship between health and the act of proper communication.

Health communication as a discipline exists on the threshold of multiple sectors because it combines scientific knowledge and findings from the life sciences, such as health, with the communication sciences, which is larger than media studies. If you go to the doctor, you do not use media; you sit there, and she sits there, and you talk. It matters to both of you whether that's a good conversation or not. If we aggregate this dyadic relationship to the health status of an entire nation, it becomes obvious that the public will benefit from living in a well-functioning health system where the members of that system can communicate effectively and learn from each other.

I am an affiliated researcher at the Charles Perkins Centre (part of an interdisciplinary research collaboration surrounding obesity prevention), a research network member on infectious disease prevention with Sydney Infectious Diseases and Biosecurity Network and an advisory board member of the International Health Humanities Network. My research is primarily in health communication, specifically in the field of community engagement, social/health practice and health humanities approaches. My plan is to get people involved in finding solutions for health behaviour maintenance as well as analysing social routine practices as determining factors for engaging in healthy behaviours, or not.

From my perspective, research needs to assist with the main objectives of professional health communication, namely creating understandable and motivational messages for the population. The one thing that we are working on is trying to figure out how we can get people to be part of an intervention as designers, co-creators or co-researchers and not just as study subjects. Moving from a position of data sources to creating their own solutions to a health challenge in their community increases the chance that targeted individuals want to make a change for good, because they have become their own solution and realise the agency and power they have over their own health.

In obesity prevention, for example, there are numerous groups and industries involved, from the accredited government agencies like hospitals and health departments to affiliated groups like dietitians and nutritionists, to self-declared experts on social and traditional media who offer up advice on diets, exercise and staying thin. In short, there are a plethora of people involved in this arena and they do not always speak the same language or have the same objective. Despite public health essentially belonging to the hard sciences – that is, it could benefit from working off unassailable evidence and data – it has, like other sciences, come under attack, with scientific knowledge represented as merely an opinion by certain players. The vaccination debates, both pre-COVID-19 on childhood immunisation as well as the recent COVID-19 vaccine confusion, serve as examples of this. Health communication is the part of public health that can train an expert how to break through the clutter and provide clear directions.

Health communication is also well positioned to connect health with its contextual factors and fields, such as politics and policy, social affairs, popular culture, and human routines. For example, the debate around the use of soft drugs like marijuana is mostly a political or social debate. Health science on how a substance impacts the brain, especially if you are under a certain age, is hardly ever the content of public or mediated discourse. Instead, arguments centre around proper policy response (too lenient, too harsh), police enforcement and control, and political and public actors speaking on behalf of an allegedly concerned public. What this example illustrates is that health is a public good that is of equal relevance to the individual and the collective. Hence, smart and effective communication matters. If we were to abrogate our own responsibilities toward our personal and community health – whether that's the result of lack of knowledge or lack of motivation – then certain power players in politics and corporations could tell us what we should do and how we should stay healthy. Alternatively, we could all be a little smarter about healthy behaviours and living a healthy life. The way we can get there is no different from any other topic, namely amassing knowledge and becoming excited about being involved. In other words, health communication research is an applied science to assist people in understanding their health in general and how they should get, and stay, healthy. It also helps to figure out who should be involved and what actions each should take.

Health communication also happens to be the area that moves health and being healthy into everyday deliberations and conversations. Despite the fact that health is a central criterion for human activity and advancement, it typically matters very little to people who are healthy; everything else, most of all having fun and living well, is more important. Health only becomes people's top priority, and sometimes their only focus, if they are seriously ill or afraid of becoming incapacitated. The only other people who think about health constantly are those who work in the sector.

For instance, drinking alcohol is not perceived by the average person as a health decision but a social one; most usually they drink with friends, and if they were to stop, they could not be with those people any longer. Moreover, to even consider this a health-related behaviour would require that people admit their drinking is leading them to ill health and risks. So, the typical arguments around health consequences of drinking are usually ignored. Communicating for better health and healthy behaviour patterns is a so-called wicked problem because we are dealing with – and sometimes restricting – someone's lifestyle choices. The messages ask people to do the opposite of what they want to do and what they are currently doing.

Since health experts tend to operate from an evidence- and outcome-oriented perspective and do not think much about the perspectives of the average member of the public, a health communication program fills the void by focusing on reaching people on their terms in order to make sure people actively contribute to getting healthy and staying healthy.

Moreover, health communication is often perceived to be the same as health promotion or marketing. But unlike commercial communication, which can focus on its specific goal of persuading target groups to purchase a particular brand, the broader challenge for health communication is that it sits next to other public topics within public communication, including social matters such as race and gender relations, environmental health, racism, chauvinism and so on. All these topics about how societies function, or don't, are not only difficult to communicate, but are also topics some segments of the population may have very different but equally committed beliefs about. Shirking away from the challenge to see the wider implications of disease and health discussions has restricted the communication of health- to data-driven promotional efforts and restricted its teaching to public health departments. In Australia, we still need to do quite a bit more cross-promoting to get the message out that health

13 Crossing disciplines to improve lives

communication exists as a distinctly different discipline to other areas in public health.

As the degree program director, I am responsible for the curriculum as a whole, as well as the four core units in the program, namely MECO6909: Crisis Communication, MECO6919: Health Communication, MECO6927: Leadership Communication, and MECO6934: Social Issues Marketing. In the very early days, though, there weren't any core courses on offer that had health or crisis in the title. Courses of that nature were taken as electives from the School of Public Health since the health communication degree was also a cross-listed master's level degree in the portfolio of postgraduate degrees for Public Health. That was my best understanding of it when I came in. Overall, the degree structure follows the pattern of all MECO postgraduate degrees: a full-time enrolled student completes the master's degree in three semesters, taking four units per semester. Those must include the four core units, a so-called capstone unit (with a practical or theoretical course choice) and roughly seven electives.

What I believe makes our degree unique is its cross-disciplinary nature, existing on the threshold between health and social sciences. As such, the degree not only offers a vast diversity of university-wide elective course choices, from public health policy to culture and gender studies, but has also implemented these in a model that suggests curriculum choices based on five career trajectories: health communication research, health promotion/marketing, health journalism/writing, health public relations/policy support, and community engagement. Our so-called pathways model assists students with finding interesting and appropriate courses for a smooth study period and helps them think about future career options along the way.

Our graduates include Clare Davies, senior account director at the marketing agency WE Communications; Jodie Wrigley, head of health and social change at the public relations firm Senate SHJ; Michaella Porter, account manager for the health team at WE Communications; Kayla Behayi, an account executive at Cube Public Relations; Jay Munro, vice president of marketing at the tech company WithYouWithMe; Kaitlyn Vette, an epidemiologist at the National Centre for Immunisation Research and Surveillance; and Jawahir Habib, a programme officer in UNICEF's Polio Outbreak Team.

Moreover, I have recently adjusted the delivery mode from a purely classroom-based delivery to a blended format where each Master of Health Communication unit is available in both fully online and in-person intensive modes. I expect this will make the degree attractive to already employed groups (approximately 30 to 40 percent of our students are already working in health communication or health communication adjacent fields) and people outside of Sydney, as they now can complete this degree from a distance or by coming to campus for short, concentrated workshops. This works equally for the integrated smaller degrees, the Graduate Diploma and Graduate Certificate, and has potential to advance to standalone courses for micro-credentials and continuing education schemes. In 2021, I also changed Organisational Communication to Leadership Communication, and changed some content and activities in the health communication program overall to make it more relevant for people in health and corporate positions. Needless to say, my research on the communication of health flows into the teaching and so the two domains will remain connected with each other.

What we witness now during the COVID-19 pandemic is that public communication of health and risks needs to

13 Crossing disciplines to improve lives

be done extremely well, so attracting those tasked with communication in the public service is a prime target. Health and public communication is a growing field, but it grows slowly. If the viral pandemic has taught us anything, it is that health communication is an increasingly important topic, and it should be better understood and done well by a diverse group of practitioners in the health sector. I am hopeful that the status and value of the health communication program will increasingly be recognised, and a degree in health communication will increasingly be seen as relevant and desirable.

We live in a time when everyone can see how important health communication has become, as every country tries to figure out how to get on top of the coronavirus and tell their population how to protect themselves from being infected. When people can see all the ramifications in many countries around the world where people are not following advice, they might take note when a health spokesperson tells them something. Most health communication is run through the government, non-government entities and not-for-profit organisations, with some commercial players as well; it is a very broad field. Considering the mistakes that these various entities (especially governments) have made – and will continue to make – in communicating clear paths out of the pandemic, it is clear that health communication is a vital field with a bright future.

14
Building confidence and courage: internships
Kiran Gupta

There are many words to describe the media industry: stable is not one of them. For many students, precarity is what comes to mind. Precarity of jobs, precarity of journalists, precarity of print media. With more and more job cuts and decreasing funding, especially in Australia, media practitioners need to fight harder and harder for their first jobs. At the University of Sydney, students have a leg-up: the internship program.

The internship may not be the first thing that students picture when envisaging their degree. To the prospective student's eye, coursework is likely seen as the hallmark of a media degree, and to an extent, this is true. The rigour and depth of learning in the coursework program provides graduates with the tools to succeed in the workforce. Only in a media degree will units that explore critical theories of race and gender be interspersed with units that make you go to court and file a report by the end of the day. The internship program, however, is another shining light in the MECO armoury. It provides students with the opportunity to intern at a firm of their choosing in the form of media they are looking to gain experience in, and to obtain credit for it.

The Bachelor of Arts and Bachelor of Advanced Studies (Media and Communications) degree at the University of Sydney is structured to build up to the internship in the final year of study. MECO1001: Introduction to Media Studies and MECO1002: Digital Media and Communications Landscapes lay the groundwork for understanding basic media theory. MECO1003 provides an introduction to the principles of media writing and MECO1004 provides an introduction to media production. From there, students are encouraged to find their niche through the exploration of a wide range of mediums with leading professionals as lecturers and tutors. These subjects include MECO2601: Audio Production, MECO2602: Video Production, MECO2604: Telling Stories with Data and MECO3606: Advanced Media Writing. After a final unit that explores the legal and ethical requirements of being in the media industry, students undertake a compulsory fourth year, where they will either pursue honours or a major media project in a discipline of their choosing. Both options include the semester-long internship.

The internship has been a formative part of the undergraduate degree since its inception in 2000. Catharine Lumby, the founder of the MECO degree and the chair of the department from 2021 to 2022, told me about the importance of having a tailor-made internship program.

"In 1999, I was hired by Sydney University to set up the entire media and communications degree," she said, "and I valued equally theoretical knowledge and professional experience. Because we wanted to be producing people who feel equipped to go into the increasingly volatile media industry."

14 Building confidence and courage

The internships reflected the variety of fields explored in the degree, spanning journalism, PR, marketing and much more, allowing students to try their hand at a wide range of media careers.

"Even in the 2000s, people went through revolving doors," said Lumby, "so in the degree I set up, all students had to do basic writing, researching, interviewing and they had to do that in print, TV, radio and online. This gave students a portfolio of skills which were flexible and transferable."

Lumby also stressed that a strength of the internship program was its intimacy: "When we started in 2000, I insisted that the course was capped at 100 students a year, so we could teach professional practice in a really intensive, high-end way."

From the outset, MECO has employed a full-time undergraduate internship coordinator. Fiona Martin described how, for the first decade, Indigo Blue and Robin Moffat deftly and empathically handled student and industry inquiries. They also ably assisted Richard Broinowski, who set up the overseas journalism fellowship program (see Chapter 15), which saw students compete for internships at major overseas media companies.

The postgraduate internship program is also a vital part of the department. Introduced from 2004, the internship is a recommended capstone unit in all five postgraduate degrees.

It is clear when speaking to members of the department how significant the internship program is. Alana Mann is particularly effusive.

"The internship is considered to be a very important element of the MECO program because it gives students that professional experience of working in the media. Media organisations can be extremely stressful and very demanding. The internship program makes sure that students are prepared and ready to hit the ground running once they enter the workforce."

Mann also noted that the structure of the program ensures students are looked after.

"Having an internship embedded in the program and one that is for credit underlines the fact that we recognise this program and the fact that you can learn a great deal. It also acknowledges the presence of a university–host relationship that provides a supportive environment and pastoral care, whereas if you went straight into the workplace, you're working with really busy people."

She said that she has seen the benefits of the internship for MECO students.

"One of the biggest assets of the program is the relationships that you develop. It's a small industry and Australia is a relatively small job market so if you look after [your relationships] and cultivate them, they'll be really valuable in the future," she said. "We've got students who are doing incredible, incredible things ... the internship gives them the confidence and the courage to chase some of those opportunities."

Examples of successful graduates of the MECO internship program can be seen all over Sydney, including through the ranks of *The Sydney Morning Herald* journalists: reporters Pallavi Singhal, Natassia Chrysanthos and Michael Koziol all benefitted from internships through the University.

Bunty Avieson and Adriana Hernandez currently coordinate the undergraduate internship program. It is a large program, with about 100 students undertaking internships each year, so Avieson handles the academic side and Hernandez handles the administrative side. Avieson has been in her role since 2016 and Hernandez since 2014, succeeding Moffat. One

14 Building confidence and courage

recent afternoon, the three of us met in Avieson's office. Every few minutes, the conversation segued into an anecdote about a past or current student.

"One student wanted to do an internship at the Human Rights Commission," Avieson said, "so Adriana contacted them and made it possible for them to intern there. They needed to design a program for us because they didn't have any media program, but we made it work."

Avieson then asked Hernandez whether the student continued to work with the Human Rights Commission.

"She stayed there part-time," Hernandez said. "That's the best marketing I have, a student staying at the place of the internship for their job."

Avieson said the University's broad coursework program makes the internship even more worthwhile.

"Every step of the way, students are encouraged to critically reflect, not just learning how to produce media content but to think about it, to consider it and to look at society and think bigger. The internship program helps students apply a critical lens to the workplace. So that it's not just work experience. It's about identifying the work culture and critically reflecting on that."

While the internship is a formative step towards employment and seen as an integral part of the MECO program, it is also seen as a place where mistakes can be made.

"They [the employers] expect a lot from students in the internship," said Hernandez, "but because it's an internship and it's supposed to be a mentoring program, you can make mistakes. You definitely can. And you're not going to get sacked, but you still learn."

Students also see the very real impact of their work, as it is often published by the organisation they are working for.

Figure 14.1 Adriana Hernandez, 2022, photo by Bill Green

"Students consistently tell us that they don't realise how much real work they are doing; for example, running the social media accounts. And their work is published. It is published in *The Sydney Morning Herald* again and again. They are shocked that they are seen as credible, but they are given responsibility so they develop confidence," Avieson said.

While students intern at a variety of places, including *The Sydney Morning Herald*, SBS, CNN and *The New York Times*,

14 Building confidence and courage

Avieson and Hernandez are quick to note it is not just journalism firms that offer an internship program.

"We work with so many different agencies because our degree is so broad," Hernandez said. "Now, it's more PR agencies and the media keeps changing and changing and we change with it. Many companies now work with influencers. I would have never thought that. So now our students are working with influencers in marketing agencies."

Avieson added, "We actually have students working with Taronga Zoo. They have an amazing media department and a lot of stuff happening, so it's not even just media organisations."

Anna Jenica Bacud is one Master of Media Practice student who has enjoyed working at a non-media organisation. Hailing from the Philippines and arriving with a diverse range of media experience from journalism to content production in her home country, Bacud wanted to do something different to further diversify her experience.

"I wanted to get out into the workforce and experience the Australian work culture for myself," she said.

She managed to secure an internship as a student media producer with the Business Co-Design team at the University of Sydney Business School. Bacud lauded the program for allowing her to develop a broad range of skills, while focusing on her primary strength: podcasting.

"They really allowed me to do what I was interested in," she said. "This started with doing little video editing projects for their social media and expanded into other short projects such as animations and blog posts. But they also encouraged me to do a long-term project, which helped me develop my skills in podcasting outside the classroom. It was invaluable and nice to do something different every day, learning from wonderfully passionate and talented people."

While the COVID-19 pandemic interfered with the internships, it also created a silver lining for Hernandez.

"All internships last year were 100 percent online. It was unique and students had to adapt to those changes."

"Some of the students were actually face to face when the internship program started, then had to go online and then came back. That's three different cultures in a single internship. That's amazing. And that makes a great journalist."

Tim Piccione was one Master of Media Practice student who managed to find a silver lining in the disruption the COVID-19 pandemic caused to the internship program.

"My internship with *SBS Insight* was postponed once and then eventually cancelled the day before I was supposed to start it due to ongoing COVID setbacks," Piccione mused. "I had the outfit laid out on the Sunday and then it was cancelled via email. It was a huge punch in the gut."

To make matters worse, after managing to get an internship with Leigh Sales's *7:30 Report* on the ABC, Piccione was again left in the lurch due to COVID-19.

"It was pushed back again and then cancelled," he said. "I was really devastated. I really let it get to me."

However, just as it seemed as if an internship was beyond the realms of possibility, Piccione found an internship with entertainment and culture digital publication *Urban List Sydney*.

"It was both a moment of thinking I should just take what I can get and accepting that although it was not what I had envisaged, there was something exciting about it," Piccione said. "It was a 'Plan C' I suppose, but it's actually turned out to be quite a good thing."

For Piccione, this ended up being an eye-opening experience, completely changing his journalism career path, which was initially focused on "hard journalism".

"At uni, you're doing a lot of theoretical writing. But getting to do the internship is what helped me learn in a practical setting. I was immediately contributing to the publication and understanding what deadlines you have to make," Piccione said. "It was definitely a wake-up call for me."

Piccione gained professional experience from his internship, and he is still writing for the publication.

"I started writing an article here and there from day one," he said. "Now I'm regularly freelancing for them. I'm now starting an online publication with a friend of mine as well. It's a bit of everything at the moment."

Even in a challenging year, Piccione was able to find an internship relevant to him.

The department is proud of the individual connection and the personal touch with their internship program. Moffat, who worked as the internship coordinator from May 2006 to May 2014, recalls it was this way from the start. She remembers interviewing students to ascertain their interest areas before finding them relevant internships. She contacted companies to see if they would be willing to host students and sometimes accompanied MECO academics to meet new clients and discuss the program. As the years passed, clients began contacting MECO asking for interns. "The program had a very good reputation in the industry," Moffat said.

Today, Hernandez continues working with each student to ensure they find a suitable placement.

Figure 14.2 Lauren Castino, 2024, photo by Sally Joas

This sometimes includes rural placements. "[Students] might want to spend January, February with their family in the country. And if we can find something, we are more than happy to accommodate that. One person, they're going to ABC Ulladulla. I'm super happy for them to do that. The experience is so amazing because it is a small unit, and they know and can write about the community. And those students will actually love to give something back to their community," Avieson said.

For Lauren Castino, who has been the postgraduate internship coordinator for nearly four years, the internship has incredible value. "The feedback from students who have found an employment path through doing the internship, I think that's the proof in the pudding."

The message from students is clear. The internship changes lives. It sets up careers and sparks imaginations. And that is what a tertiary education is all about.

Bacud sums it up best: "Without the internship, I don't know where I would be."

15
From *The Korea Herald* to the *Bangkok Post*: Overseas Fellowship Program

Weien Su and Cheryl O'Byrne

One January day in 2011, Hamish Boland-Rudder travelled from Sydney to Seoul. It was 40°C when he got on the plane and -17°C when he got off. He was unprepared for the Korean chill and had to dig through his bag at the airport to find some warm clothes.

Back then, Boland-Rudder was a final year Bachelor of Arts (Media and Communications) student at the University of Sydney. He applied to MECO's Overseas Fellowship Program and was selected as an Australia Korea Foundation Fellow for 2011. A few months later, he arrived, cold, to begin work as a media intern at *The Korea Herald*.

The Overseas Fellowship Program began in 2004 with Richard Broinowski's idea to send media students to work at English-language newspapers and other media organisations in Asia. Broinowski had a long career as a diplomat with the Department of Foreign Affairs and Trade (DFAT) and served as general manager of Radio Australia in the early 1990s. After retiring from DFAT in 1998, he became an adjunct professor in

Inside stories

Figure 15.1 Overseas Fellowship Program fellow Hamish Boland-Rudder in *The Korea Herald* office, 2011, photo courtesy of Hamish Boland-Rudder

Media Studies at the University of Canberra. Three years later, he assumed the same position at the University of Sydney.

Broinowski used the contacts he gained as a diplomat to develop the program. In its first year, then called Media Students to Asia, he sent two students to Bangkok: one to the *Bangkok Post* and the other to *The Nation*. Over the next year or two, he extended the host outlets to include *The Phnom Penh Post*, *The Cambodia Daily*, *The Star* (Malaysia), a television channel in Kuala Lumpur, and the *Philippine Daily Enquirer*. Around 2010, he expanded the program to include *Korea JoongAng Daily*, *The Korea Herald* and TBS Radio in

15 From The Korea Herald to the Bangkok Post

Seoul; *Global Times*, *Beijing Review* and *Caixin* in Beijing; and *Agence France-Presse* in Tokyo. Broinowski recalls that MECO academic Fiona Martin and MECO undergraduate program internship coordinator Robin Moffat accompanied him on a "setting-up" trip to meet with the editors in these three cities. Thereafter, he added newspapers in the United Arab Emirates, India and Santiago, Chile.

Broinowski tells us he was initially motivated by experiences he had during his career that exposed the ignorance some Australian journalists had when it came to Asia. He wanted "to imbue [students] with sophisticated experiences that they would not get from being mere tourists in Asia."

These motivations accord with the current objectives of the Overseas Fellowship Program. Adriana Hernandez, who has been internship coordinator since 2014, explains that the program improves the quality and sophistication of Australian media reporting overseas, and promotes the bilateral relationships between Australia and other countries. Students undergo a competitive application process. Each year of her tenure, the department has received 20 to 25 applications and offered 12 to 15 fellowships.

Boland-Rudder describes his time working and living in Korea as "a mind-blowing experience, both in terms of the journalistic challenge and the opportunities of exploring a whole new country."

The language barrier didn't stop him from creating good content. He built a network of sources by calling people who could speak English and asking them to help him navigate the local media landscape and the city.

He published "Americans' lifelong love of Korean music" in *The Korea Herald* on 10 February 2011. The story featured a 79-year-old American medic who mastered the art of playing the Korean gayageum. Boland-Rudder remembers how difficult it was jumping on a train alone and finding where he needed to go without Google Maps or a smartphone. He also remembers sitting in the man's apartment listening to music together. "It felt like a real privilege and a real moment of meeting fascinating people and doing things I never otherwise do," he said. "This is one of the joys of journalism."

Boland-Rudder identifies *The Korea Herald* fellowship as a formative moment in his career. He is now an online editor at the International Consortium of Investigative Journalists. He works with more than 400 journalists from 80 different countries on one to two big stories each year. His experience in Korea had a significant impact on landing a job with this cross-border organisation. The experience opened his mind to the possibility of working in media outside Australia. It enabled him to work with reporters from different cultural backgrounds and taught him how to go about finding stories in a completely unfamiliar world.

Another lesson Boland-Rudder learned was giving everything a go in both career and life. Trying kimchi for the first time, hiking up a mountain outside Seoul and publishing his first news story were all part of his unique experiences in Korea. "The whole experience taught me the power of just saying yes and trying everything," he said.

Broinowski tells us that all host editors agreed fellows would be treated as journalists. For a four- to eight-week attachment they could choose their own stories, do the research and get published. One drawcard for the editors was that this was free labour. The fellowship covered airfares and a living stipend. Initially, Broinowski obtained funding from the Myer Foundation in Melbourne. Baillieu Myer, a businessman and philanthropist, was a friend. By 2010, funding was coming directly from DFAT.

Lydia Feng is another alumna who participated in the Overseas Fellowship Program. While undertaking her Bachelor of Arts (Media and Communications) degree, Feng chose politics and international studies units as her electives. She found herself passionate about becoming a journalist, especially one who would report on world news and politics.

A few years after Boland-Rudder, she became an Australia–China Council Fellow for 2014 and worked as a media intern in Beijing with *Caixin Media*. Working alongside senior journalists and editors, she was able to put theories she learned from university into practice. During her time there, she attended a press conference on the World Economic Forum, created a feature spread on the Shanghai Free Trade Zone, wrote an article about the Beijing Art Exhibition and reviewed a book.

"Working overseas at the leading media company has given me confidence in my abilities and inspired me to work as a journalist overseas someday," she posted to *Parallax*, the blog that fellows contributed to during their placements.

The fellowship program ensures that future Australian journalists have an in-depth understanding of foreign cultures, politics and history. The fellow's placement is preceded by a debrief at the Australian Embassy/Consulate in the host country. Feng spent her first week at the Australian Embassy in Beijing discussing the current economic and political climate in

Figure 15.2 Richard Broinowski at his farewell party in 2014

China and its impact on Sino–Australian relations. The week affirmed her fascination with international affairs.

In Feng's spare time, she immersed herself in China's rich culture, visiting the country's most iconic landmarks from the Forbidden City to the Great Wall. Her Chinese heritage made her feel even more interested in and connected to the country.

"Walking ten thousand miles of the world is better than reading ten thousand scrolls of books," Feng posted to the blog, quoting an old Chinese proverb. Being the new kid on the Beijing block was not as daunting as she had imagined. Though she stumbled her way through many Chinese conversations at the time, she knew this allowed her to practise her Mandarin.

Her internship in Beijing wasn't just a chance to familiarise herself with Chinese culture and meet Chinese journalists; she also met people from all over the world who shared the same

15 From The Korea Herald to the Bangkok Post

passions, including people who were interning from other countries. "It was good to have that international perspective and great to see they [former colleagues] are flourishing now in their careers in various countries," she told us.

Feng's experience of working in an overseas media organisation enabled her to apply and expand her knowledge in news writing and had a significant impact on her career. After graduation, she earned a competitive SBS cadetship and then worked as a reporter at SBS for several years. Feng is now a reporter for *ABC News Sydney* with a focus on local communities, world politics and immigration. Speaking over Zoom from her ABC office, it seems she has achieved the goals that she set herself while at university. "The fellowship was undoubtedly a rewarding experience," she said.

The same year that Feng headed to China, Mikaela Griffith was selected as a 2014 Australia Thailand Institute Fellow. She spent five weeks in Thailand, with one week at the Australian Embassy and four weeks at the *Bangkok Post*.

At the Australian Embassy, she worked in the Public Diplomacy Unit, writing and editing press releases and having briefings with various organisations including Australian Education International and the Australian Trade Commission. She gained experience in public relations and saw many ways Australia was working to strengthen the bilateral relationship with Thailand. Working and living in Thailand allowed her to experience the culture of the country as more than a tourist.

During her time at the *Bangkok Post*, Griffith worked as a lifestyle writer and reporter. Her role involved researching and pitching article ideas, conducting interviews and writing stories across a wide range of topics.

Griffith published seven articles at the newspaper and participated in a range of projects at the embassy. Her experiences in Thailand gave her the chance to practise her journalism skills and gave her great insights into the local media landscape. In a *Parallax* blog post, she described the day she opened up Tuesday's Lifestyle section of the *Bangkok Post* and saw her name in print: "I actually let out a squeak of excitement and did a little dance, a big silly grin all over my face."

"One of the most valuable things this fellowship gave me was a stronger sense of confidence, in both myself and my ability as a professional journalist," Griffith wrote.

Seven years later, Griffith names the fellowship program one of her "most cherished life experiences to date." In an email from Amsterdam, where she has lived and worked since 2019, Griffith wrote, "My MECO studies and overseas fellowship undoubtedly armed me with lifelong skills that have helped me adapt and succeed in this international environment."

After completing her degree, Griffith studied design thinking at Politecnico di Milano, Italy. She began working as a copywriter for the global advertising agency Ogilvy, and she is now a content writer at the global headquarters of Adyen, a Dutch financial technology company that has 26 offices around the world, from São Paulo to Tokyo. "International collaboration is an integral part of my job," she wrote, "from supporting local offices … to navigating the cultural nuances of our blog's diverse global audience." One of her recent projects was a case study with the Rijksmuseum that will be translated for local markets around the world.

15 From The Korea Herald to the Bangkok Post

The fellowship "has had a lasting, positive influence on me both personally and professionally, from building my confidence to inspiring me to continually seek out new challenges and opportunities around the world," she wrote.

Close to 200 graduates, like Boland-Rudder, Feng and Griffith, have participated in the fellowship program. The program has continued to help the next generation of Australian journalists gain a better understanding of other countries while also helping other countries gain a better understanding of Australia. Students have acquired knowledge and professional skills in different countries and media landscapes. They are applying their international perspectives and developing a sophisticated approach to their own media work.

The fellowship program has been paused since 2020, due to changes in funding by DFAT and the COVID-19 pandemic. Bunty Avieson, the MECO academic who runs the program, is looking forward to its full restoration. In the meantime, MECO has resumed a partnership with the Korean Australian Community Support Incorporation, sending 11 final year students to Korea for an immersion program in 2022, with another group scheduled to go in 2023. MECO's collaboration with the Australian Consortium for "In-Country" Indonesian Studies recently enabled two students to intern at Metro TV and *The Jakarta Post*.

The Overseas Fellowship Program "puts students right at the heart of what is going on in a foreign country," Avieson said. She has witnessed the way this enables students "to understand different cultures and how the media best serves their communities". It is "an extraordinary opportunity that changes lives".

16
"A critical part of the MECO family": higher degree research students

Agata Mrva-Montoya and Penny O'Donnell

Kim McNamara was Catharine Lumby's first PhD student. She enrolled in 1999 and researched the world of celebrities, paparazzi, social media and brand cultures. As Lumby recalled, "In the early days of the department, we worked collaboratively to build a strong research culture. We intentionally wanted to be working with people who were committed to research and who were emerging researchers."

At the beginning, the MECO Higher Degree Research (HDR) program attracted mainly mid-career journalists and people in other areas of media and communications who had worked in the industry but wanted to complete a PhD and move into academia. As Lumby said, "It was the beginning in a shift towards seeing media and communications as a research-driven discipline, not just a vocation. Though the vocational and professional aspects are very important. A lot of the PhDs were ones that integrated reflection on professional practice and brought that into the research space."

Megan Le Masurier's thesis about *Cleo* magazine, which she started in 2000, was typical of the kind of PhD that Lumby and later her colleagues started to supervise. As a senior editor at a women's magazine and a feminist, Le Masurier was interested in exploring the idea that some feminists saw women's magazines as always trivial and sexist. Lumby recounted the project: "And Megan said, 'no, it's more complicated than that'. She went back and researched the early years of *Cleo* magazine, which Ita Buttrose edited, and she said that actually *Cleo* was a feminist magazine. It just talked about it in popular terms. It was in the early days in the 70s, where average women in Australia who wouldn't identify as feminist were curious about, what is this women's liberation, how will it affect my life? So to me it is an example of really important historically archival research that takes a popular magazine seriously, and says it did real work in real women's lives. While the 'radical women' who marched on the streets were crucial to the feminist movement, they weren't always presenting their message in a relatable way. Cleo 'translated feminism for a much broader audience'."

For Lumby, the objective in the early days of the HDR program was to bring together a group of talented research students, like Le Masurier and McNamara, give them resources, mentor and support them, and allow a research culture to develop. As MECO was forging a new space in communications research, "what happened was rhizomatic – networks and different branches of ideas formed organically throughout. And HDR students were a critical part of the MECO family. We involved them and engaged them in research projects, and brainstorming sessions about what was this research culture? What were we doing in this space?"

The life of an HDR student, and their supervisor, was different in the early 2000s compared to now. Academics were allowed a lot more discretion and the supervision process was far less bureaucratic. Lumby said, "This was easier for the supervisor and easier for the student. And I think it allowed us to spend more time on the actual work of making the PhD happen. These days students frequently complain to me, and maybe to other academics, that they spend a lot of time reporting and filling in paperwork. And they prefer to be working on their work." While she recognised the benefits of greater accountability, she added, "More generally, we've become very corporatised. And that means that there are a lot of layers of bureaucracy to everything that we do. And sometimes that can get in the way of doing the work. It actually puts some people off doing a PhD, which is a shame, because ultimately it's a creative work. It's a brave endeavour, and it's a journey that the supervisor and the students embark on together. And there's no one size fits all to supervision. People work differently. They have different needs. They need different kinds of support." The scholarships available at the university level were always scarce and competitive, hence most MECO HDR students did not receive one – a situation that continues today.

Pastoral support was a key element of the HDR supervision. While there was less bureaucracy to contend with in the early days of MECO, HDR students had the usual universal challenges associated with working on a huge project, which affects a significant part of student life and impacts their family and friends. Lumby, Anne Dunn and Steven Maras worked closely on supporting students through the process. This was particularly important for those younger students who came straight out of an undergraduate degree. Apart from the cohort of industry professionals, the HDR program also drew on the strong, academically gifted honours cohort.

Lumby said they always worked "from the person to the thesis", not the other way around. She added, "I think that philosophy is still there in the MECO department, that we are academically rigorous, but we put people first and that to me is at the heart of good supervision and at the heart of caring for our HDR community, because I see them as our colleagues, and therefore, they need to be listened to and often they're doing research at the cutting edge of where the field is going. So, we learn from them."

As MECO grew, the HDR program evolved. A role of HDR coordinator was established to administer the program effectively, which meant helping students progress while maintaining good relations with supervisors. HDR coordinators scheduled reviews and organised events to facilitate the progress of HDR students to completion. The role was undertaken first by Dunn, followed by Maras (2007–11), Penny O'Donnell (2011–13), Joyce Nip (2014–16), Benedetta Brevini (2017–19) and, more recently, Jonathon Hutchinson (2019–22).

Dunn had an unerring capacity to recruit high-quality candidates. Maras organised the administration of policy, degree information, admissions, supervision, communications, submission and examination with characteristic verve and diligence. He set up a mini-conference in 2007 to coincide with annual reviews. The conference provided an occasion for students to share their research with their peers and the broader MECO community.

O'Donnell took the role in a new direction, by introducing fortnightly "research-in-conversation" meetings to increase HDR communicational skills development. Students were

16 "A critical part of the MECO family"

Figure 16.1 Benedetta Brevini, 2022, photo by Stefanie Zingsheim

invited to set the agenda by nominating the themes, readings or issues they wanted to discuss and, within a short timeframe, the HDR research culture became more collegial and intellectually rewarding. Some examples of topics covered include "The pace and flow of academic writing", "Your PhD is a career", "Embracing the challenge of becoming a writer",

"Ten tips for failing a PhD", "The bibliography challenge", "How not to write a thesis", "The ethics of research", "The university as an intellectual community", "Peer review", "How to apply for a Postgraduate Research Support grant", "Planning the end game", "Social media and PhD research", "Research principles", and the all-time favourite topic, "Dancing and wrestling with scholarship".[1]

By the 2012 end-of-year HDR mini-conference, many students were better-placed to present a 20-minute research presentation. That was a great outcome. O'Donnell was invited, along with Gerard Goggin (then head of department), to run an "enhancing graduate culture" workshop for the School of Literature, Arts and Media (SLAM).

During Nip's time as HDR coordinator, she sought to refine MECO's approach to the required Postgraduate Research Annual Progress Reviews. Nip added a second, mid-year annual review, held in conjunction with an additional mini-conference, to better administer the probation of students who start their studies in the middle of the academic year. She also organised orientation briefings and welcome events for new students, as well as workshops on special topics targeted at students at different stages of candidature (in addition to University-wide initiatives such as HDR Student Connect Event and Pitch Perfect: Present Your Thesis in 3 Minutes).

Following the merge of MECO and Digital Cultures in 2013, bringing together research students with diverse topic interests became a priority. As Brevini said, from a theoretical and methodological perspective it was easy to merge them. But the merge required a framework to make it happen. Brevini

---

1   Back, 2002.

also wanted to create a stronger connection between the honours program, master's by research and the PhD program.

As the department grew, the HDR enrolments grew too. As noted earlier, the first two PhD students started in 1999 and 2000; they were joined by the first master's by research student a year later. The first three students graduated in 2006. The numbers grew each year and in 2010, there were 24 PhD students and nine master's students going through the program. Two years later, in 2012, MECO recorded its highest number of students, with 40 HDR enrolled candidates in total. This number dropped to a low of 21 students in 2020 and rose again to 29 in 2022. The first international master's student started in 2006, and the first three international PhD students started in 2007. Since then, MECO has enrolled international students of 18 nationalities, with the greatest numbers coming from China, followed by Indonesia, the UK, New Zealand, Germany and India.

To improve communication with a growing cohort of students, and create a sense of community, Nip set up an email list and eCommunity site on Blackboard. Building on these initiatives, Brevini established a mandatory research seminar held fortnightly, at which students would give updates on their own work and hear from MECO staff and guest speakers about the intricacies of conference planning, abstract writing and becoming a researcher. She also encouraged HDR students to attend the Media@Sydney seminar series to further participate in the research culture of the department.

Brevini also played a pivotal role in replacing the two small mini-conferences associated with the reviews with an annual conference for HDR students. "So everybody had to be there. Everybody had to present the paper. Everybody had to come to support their peers. And in this way, everybody knew that the conference was happening in November, they could plan towards it." It was another opportunity to strengthen the HDR community, because as Brevini said, "University is not just about making people job ready. It's about teaching them how to be humans and teaching them how to be citizens, how to be together in a community that is separated from the market and is not judged only on market values but it is judged on what you're bringing, how you can enrich yourself; the kind of knowledge you can share and affect."

Another initiative that aimed to foster closer working relationships among students and staff was the MECO HDR Pomodoro writing group that Hutchinson initiated in November 2019. The idea was to have a mix of academics and HDR students from MECO attending, but generally the meetings attracted more students than staff. Hutchinson wanted this to be a student-led initiative, so invited Michael Ward and Agata Stepnik to take over the organisation and hosting duties. The group initially met in person, but since the COVID-19 lockdowns in April–May 2020, the meetings have been conducted online. Hutchinson also experimented with fortnightly research symposium/book clubs, giving students a chance to have their work read, for all to work on an article, chapter or book together, and to update each other on research developments in the previous fortnight.

While these initiatives were developed at the departmental level, in the background the University was working on reforms to introduce coursework, streamline the administrative process and manage the HDR cohort, which became the HDR Policy 2020. Inspired by the model coming from the Faculty of Science, the University wanted to require PhD students to complete two units to develop their research skills. While in theory this model was a great idea, Brevini found the timing problematic. She said, "it is all good that they are trained, but they should be trained before they start the PhD because in three years, they won't have enough time for both coursework and research". Nevertheless, the coursework became compulsory for students from 2021.

The University also introduced a compulsory supervisor training course, a University-wide register of supervisors, and the need to have co-supervised two master's or PhD students to completion before they can take a lead supervisor role. Moreover, supervisors cannot take on more than five concurrent students.

A new University-wide online system to improve the administration of reviews was trialled at MECO in 2017, which has since been replaced by a new system. While there are efficiency benefits in having a central platform, the trend towards centralisation had been opposed by many academics in the Faculty of Arts and Social Sciences who saw the disciplinary differences as a problem for managing the reviews. Eventually, the school decided to have a layer of reviews managed at the departmental level, as disciplinary knowledge is critical for recruitment of new HDR students, though most of the coordination is managed at the school level as part of the new policy. While the MECO HDR coordinator previously filtered out enquiries on topics unrelated to research done at MECO before sending them out to colleagues to find a suitable supervisor, these days a MECO HDR Admissions Committee reviews applications. This collective effort aims to improve the quality of applicants and align the HDR intake with the research trajectory of the department by targeting areas that MECO is interested in pursuing.

Not everyone sees the effort to follow a specific research agenda as a positive development though. Brevini pointed to a difference between the way a department and a research institute should operate. "If you're working in a research institute, it's all well and fine to push through the research agenda of the institute. But if you work in a department, you should pursue diversity of research."

Not surprisingly, as the diversity of research interest among MECO staff has increased, the range of HDR topics has grown as well. At the beginning, there was a lot of research in media and journalism. Over time, as staff in Digital Cultures expanded, students started doing more research on video games, for example, which Brevini saw as a positive development. "If you have a diverse cohort of expertise, then you can take different PhD students. But the discipline in terms of the theory, the theoretical aspects and the methodology, are still the same. So when we train them, we train them with the same tools."

Over the years, MECO has hosted numerous outstanding HDR students who have gone on to successful careers in academia and beyond. For example, Christy Dena (2009) investigated the nature of transmedia practice in her PhD. She is a storyteller, educator and researcher, and currently part-time professor of cross-media and interactive narratives at the Norwegian Film School. Joe Brennan (2014), a highly acclaimed photographer and writer, looked at theory and practice of slash manips, visual fan works that layer images of male characters from popular media with gay material. Lukasz Swiatek (2015) looked at the world of accolades such as the Nobel Prize as media and communications entities; he is now a lecturer in the School of the Arts and Media at UNSW. Lucy Watson (2019) investigated celebrity culture and the ways in which LGBTQ+ Australians read celebrity media. She is now policy and development officer at ACON, a health-promotion organisation specialising in HIV prevention and support and LGBTQ+ health. Cherry Baylosis (2021) interrogated the potential of voice in digital media for people living with mental illness. She is now working as a policy officer with Disability Advocacy NSW.

In October 2021, Marcus Carter, Goggin and Ben Egliston were successful in securing the FASS HDR Scholarship for their project exploring VR and disability as part of the Mixed Reality Ethics Project and the Socio-Tech Futures Lab. This was a welcome development in the otherwise bleak two years of the pandemic, which saw many HDR students struggle to continue their studies. Some couldn't pursue their research in lockdowns because they had extra caring responsibilities or other hindrances. Many missed out on opportunities to travel to conferences and network. All students were permitted to extend their candidature by six months.

The work on finetuning the HDR processes has continued. At the end of February 2021, the Annual Progress Review process was retired and replaced by Progress Evaluations, with specific progression milestones. The role of HDR coordinator at the departmental level has been replaced by school HDR coordinators tasked with remaining in close contact with MECO students, including all pastoral care. The focus remains on building a strong research community and culture.

Works cited

Back, L. (2002). Dancing and wrestling with scholarship: Things to do and things to avoid in a PhD career. *Sociological Research Online*, 7(4), 16–20. https://doi.org/10.5153/sro.764

17
Enlarging perspectives: networks of domestic research partnerships

Jenny Welsh

"So, what does food have to do with media and communications?" I am talking to Alana Mann, academic in MECO (now at the University of Tasmania) and co-founder of FoodLab Sydney, about her most recent research project, and this is my burning question.

Mann tells me she gets asked this a lot and that food is *everything* to do with communication. "I think food has a huge communication problem because there is so much misinformation," she says. "We've got to have a more democratic food system and to do that we've got to inform people about what's going on."

Mann has spent much of her career researching social movement campaigns and the politics around food. Her latest book, *Food in a changing climate,* addresses the relationship between food and climate change, and how hyper-consumerism and complex food chains have contributed to damaging our environment.

"Media and communications people have the skills and understanding of how you create accessible material for different audiences. I'm really interested in the power in food systems, and I'm equally interested in the power in media systems."

MECO academics have initiated numerous multidisciplinary research projects that apply their media and communications expertise to areas as diverse as food systems, film, robotics, healthcare, urban design, e-safety, the climate emergency and political lobbying. Often these projects involve collaborations with international partners (as described in Chapter 18). In this chapter, we'll look at some recent examples of collaborations that have relied upon domestic partnerships, such as Mann's FoodLab Sydney, which launched in 2019 and is a joint venture between the University of Sydney, the City of Sydney, FoodLab Detroit (on which it is modelled) and TAFE NSW.

Mann co-founded the Australian Research Council (ARC) funded project through her involvement with the Sydney Environment Institute, which is a multidisciplinary institute that brings together researchers from different parts of the University. At the heart of the project is the desire to create more equitable and sustainable food systems, and to give those who are marginalised or food insecure the opportunity to become part of the food industry. Mann describes FoodLab as a "food business incubator": in other words, an education and training program for those eager to start a career in food.

FoodLab promotes collaborations with people from all walks of life, including industry leaders, academics and City of Sydney residents. The involvement of academic researchers has enabled a focus on data collection, analysis and evaluation.

The project has so far helped more than 70 food entrepreneurs in the three years it was funded and continues to enhance the diversity of the food systems in Sydney's inner

17 Enlarging perspectives

city as an independent entity. As a director on the board of this new social enterprise, Mann hopes that FoodLab will continue to be part of the Sydney foodscape. She would also like to see the model rolled out in other local government areas and cities across Australia.

Diana Chester is a lecturer in media production at MECO and has worked on collaborative research in the area of environmental humanities and data sonification with the Sydney Environment Institute and the Sydney Nano Institute. She is director of *Pandemic Vibrations*, a project that explores the soundscapes of the COVID-19 pandemic and considers their impact on people's emotional and physical wellbeing. In this project, Chester collaborated with Benjamin Carey, lecturer in composition and music technology at Sydney Conservatorium of Music, Melody Li, lecturer in animation at UNSW, and two Sydney-based musicians, Julian Bel-Bachir and Sonya Holowell, to tell a story through a mix of animation, music and sound design.

Chester tracked the journey through the pandemic from when the news first broke of the virus in Wuhan and people's lives were upturned by daily media reports, to when the panic began to subside as vaccines became available. With funding from the City of Sydney and the Sydney Environment Institute, they recruited local students Sarnai Gan-Erdene, Saransh Agrawal and Abhimanyu Gupta, who created short pieces of animated film alongside the musical composition. *Pandemic Vibrations* was showcased as part of an installation at Gallery 25, ECU Galleries in Western Australia in September–October 2022.

Chester has been involved in collaborative projects since joining MECO in 2018. In 2019, they joined the Sydney

Figure 17.1 Diana Chester, 2024, photo by Stefanie Zingsheim

Nanoscience Institute as an Early Career Research Ambassador. Later that year, they were awarded a three-year Catalyst grant for her project, *Nanoresonance*, which brings together scientists and scholars from creative fields to explore the possibilities and learnings from sonifying and visualising scientific data. Together with colleagues Benjamin Carey from the Sydney Conservatorium of Music and Luke Hespanhol from the School of Architecture, Design and Planning, *Nanoresonance* has been in partnership with *Nanorobotics for Health*, a Grand Challenge project led by Anna Waterhouse from the Cardiovascular Medical Devices Group at the Charles Perkins Centre and Shelley Wickham from the Schools of Chemistry and Physics. It investigates the use of

17 Enlarging perspectives

nanotechnology in the form of nanoscale robots that can navigate the body and diagnose early disease.

"We're interested in the sort of knowledge that gets created through that process," says Chester. "It's a creative arts outcome process project where we're developing material, and then we exhibit that work. It's also a collaboration around what new knowledge can come from this and understanding the interdisciplinary nature of that research." With Carey, they have set up an artist-in-residence program at the Nano Institute to support a commitment to further collaborations between art, creativity and science.

Olaf Werder is another MECO academic who has been involved in interdisciplinary collaborative projects since he started at MECO. After joining the global advisory board of the International Health Humanities Network, Werder created Health Humanities Australia, a LinkedIn-based discussion group, and formed a collaboration with colleagues at the University of Canberra. In late 2016, he was instrumental in creating a research node with the same name at the University of Sydney's Charles Perkins Centre (CPC).

The impetus for creating the Health Humanities Australia node, and including as many disciplines in health promotion research as possible, was the idea that health is everybody's business. "This includes not just health experts and policymakers and people in labs who find solutions for medical issues, but those who are stricken by a disease or illness, those who care for them, their friends," Werder explains. The node brings together scholars from various disciplinary backgrounds, medical and health professionals, carers and creative practitioners with the aim of incorporating arts, the humanities, and social science ideas and approaches into health and wellbeing programs. As examples, Werder highlights the benefits of music or art therapy on mental health outcomes, or how hospitals should turn to architecture to become places of rest and relaxation, rather than medical factories, to give people opportunities to heal. The development of the new research node at CPC has added MECO to the list of departments involved in the centre's research and opened new methodological approaches for research projects and funding applications.

Having recently completed a funded research project on health and risk behaviour during travel (connected to infectious disease prevention behaviour) with members of the South Eastern Sydney Local Health District of NSW Health, Werder is commencing talks with colleagues from MECO, Health, Education and Engineering to collaborate on research projects in the Brain and Mind Centre, as well as in a cooperative research effort called Care Economy. All these collaborations show not only the inherently interdisciplinary nature of dealing with a population's health, but the essential role media and communications plays in it.

Olga Boichak is part of another multidisciplinary partnership at the University: the Social Media and Data Science Group, which includes Tristram Alexander (Physics), Eduardo G. Altmann (Maths and Statistics), Monika Bednarek (Linguistics) and Andrew Ross (Education). Their project has received funding from the Centre for Translational Data Science to look at connections between social media and the Black Summer bushfires of 2019–20.

Using language analysis, the researchers are looking for insights into the use of social media for communication during crises and strategies for detecting and mitigating the harmful effects of disinformation and polarisation in future climate emergencies. Boichak explains that the group is looking at the

17 Enlarging perspectives

impact of extreme weather events on public discourse; in this case, how, and to what extent, the Australian bushfires affected how people talk about climate change online and whether people have changed their opinion on the issue as a result.

Justine Humphry is chief investigator of "Emerging online safety issues: Co-creating social media education with young people", a project that aims to create online tools in partnership with young people to promote the safe use of digital technologies. Boichak and Jonathon Hutchinson are co-investigators. The project is funded through the Online Safety Grants Program administered by the eSafety Commissioner.

The project began in December 2021 and will proceed in three stages. The team has conducted online focus groups and co-designed workshops with young people aged 12–17 and their parents and carers to understand emerging online safety practices, family approaches to online rules and agreements, and perspectives on changes to online privacy through new legal regulation. Humphry explains the aim is "to identify key priorities and themes and understandings of current, really pressing issues of online safety, as perceived by those groups". The second stage will be delivering a national survey to 1,200 young people and parents. That survey will capture and delve deeper into patterns informed by priority areas identified in the focus groups, and the third stage will be producing social media education resources, which will be evaluated by students in one of MECO's social media units.

The main goal of this project is to include young people throughout its stages, in the research, design and production of any resources created. "I'm hoping there will be an avenue for young people to get their voice out, their priorities out, on the kinds of issues for them in relation to the things that make them feel unsafe, but also the strategies they have to feel safe in an online environment," Humphry says.

The team is achieving this through collaboration with Youth Action, NSW, a not-for-profit community advocacy network, and Student Edge, one of the largest member-based student organisations in Australia that specialises in youth research. Humphry explains that Student Edge specialises in supporting research with young people with "a large panel of over 95,000 members with access to a large pool of young people throughout NSW, a big network."

The team's other partner, Youth Action, NSW, has been representing young people in New South Wales for many years. The network is helping the team reach out to culturally and linguistically diverse young people, including Aboriginal and Torres Strait Islander participants.

The team is also working with Mabel Truong, a peer participation officer employed by Youth Action to work on the project one day a week. She is a student at the University, and her role is to help reach out to and engage young people in the project.

The work is upturning researchers' expectations. Humphry tells me, "We're already learning a lot just from the focus groups on how much young people already know about online safety, and that in fact, the primary need for education is actually parents, not young people."

During his time at MECO, Mitchell Hobbs has been involved in several collaborative projects that have also provided insights into the use and consequences of communication technologies. His research has focused on public lobbying strategies, social media and misinformation campaigns, and the use of dating apps.

17 Enlarging perspectives

Hobbs is currently working with colleagues from the National University of Singapore to research the use of Artificial Intelligence in strategic communication campaigns. This work focuses on how such technologies can covertly monitor and distribute messages to undermine rationality and the policy-making process in democracies. A second project currently underway focuses on public lobbying campaigns conducted by the fossil fuel industry and is a collaboration with Øyvind Ihlen from the University of Oslo.

Hobbs is also a member of the Sydney Initiative for Truth (SIFT), an interdisciplinary team that looks at the threats posed by "post-truth" phenomena such as fake news, "alternative facts" and lying. Hobbs's recent project on the suspected astroturfing campaign for the Adani Carmichael coalmine on Twitter was funded by a grant from the Sydney Post-Truth Initiative, of which David Schlosberg from the Sydney Environment Institute is a founding member. SIFT brings together researchers in linguistics, philosophy, medicine and health, politics and international relations, media and communications, psychology, and data science.[1]

These projects are only a small cross-section of the numerous research collaborations that have been taking place across the department. At first glance, they may appear to be dissimilar, but communication, in its many forms and shapes, is clearly the common ground. Communication has a critical role in many of the current challenges we face: climate change and food insecurity, digital inclusion, misinformation, big data and even health outcomes.

---

1   See more at https://web.archive.org/web/20201029185103/ https://sydneyinitiativefortruth.org/team/.

Those involved in research at MECO have set the bar high in terms of what they can achieve. In doing so, they are pushing the boundaries of communications research and how collaborations within this area are defined.

Gerard Goggin was instrumental in establishing this standard. He was an early instigator of foundational research collaborations in the area of digital media and technology, which have left significant legacies. Goggin's ARC Australian Research Fellowship on mobile phone culture (awarded in 2004) supported the convening of the first international conference on mobile media in 2007, with now Distinguished Professor Larissa Hjorth (RMIT). The conference created a network of national researchers, notably a number of doctoral and early career researchers who have become leading figures in this field. In 2006, Goggin and Kate Crawford received an award for their Mobile Media and Youth Culture in Australia project, which allowed Crawford to take up a prestigious ARC Postdoctoral Fellowship. Goggin also served as convenor of the Cultural Technologies node of the important ARC-funded Cultural Research Network (2004–09), which was able to support highly influential work in the Australian scene such as the Listening project on the media and cultural politics, in which Penny O'Donnell and Crawford were key participants.

Goggin brought longstanding ties to media policy and advocacy communities into play in MECO collaborations. He was a founding board member of the peak body Australia Communications Consumer Action Network (ACCAN), and served on their Grants Panel – as have various other MECO staff, such as Tim Dwyer and Fiona Martin.

Goggin, working with other colleagues at the University of Sydney (such as Dinesh Wadiwel in Sociology) forged research collaborations with disability communities, organisers and

17 Enlarging perspectives

policymakers, putting MECO in the vanguard of this emerging area. In 2014, Goggin was awarded an ARC Future Fellowship on disability, digital technology, rights and accessible design, which hosted a suite of workshops, conferences and conversations with a cross-section of key players in the disability field.

According to Hobbs, academics can sometimes be at risk of falling into "groupthink", where those within the same field develop similar frameworks of thinking. "Working with collaborators is a good way to make sure you're looking at issues and phenomena from multiple perspectives. So there's a resource aspect to that, but there's also the intellectual benefits of working with other minds."

18
Going global: the internationalisation of MECO

Pam Walker

The 21st century is arguably the era of peak globalisation. Our use of transnational communications platforms is consolidating the internationalisation of finance, trade and culture that began centuries earlier, and we're seeing global problems like climate change and the spread of disinformation worsening. A globalised world also needs to share its decentralised knowledge, creating new opportunities for internationalised education and necessitating more culturally sensitive approaches to learning, teaching and research.

This chapter explores how MECO has responded to these challenges, and the strategies staff have adopted to make the most of the opportunities that "going global" has presented. The department has embraced rapid changes in the curriculum, an increase in international student enrolments, and greater research collaboration with academics and academic institutions worldwide.

Gerard Goggin noted that MECO established its international research reputation over the course of its first decade, especially in areas such as digital media studies, media policy and the nascent area of journalism studies. In its 20th year, the department has become an influential research destination for international academics and a popular choice for international students, particularly from China and the Asian region.

"At its inception in 2000, MECO was focused on the national scene, and where it fitted, as a relative latecomer to media and communications in Australian universities," Goggin said. "In the intervening two decades MECO has become notably more international – not just because of the growing internationalisation and globalisation of universities in Australia and worldwide (rudely interrupted by the COVID-19 pandemic). Rather, especially because MECO's bearings and interests – especially in research – deepened in their international character and nature as the department grew in international reach and influence. In addition, media and communications as a field has internationalised significantly (if unevenly) in the last two decades, and Australian researchers have both led and taken advantage of this."

Goggin noted that MECO increasingly nurtured a disposition for multicultural, cosmopolitan and international research, especially via scholars with interests in the Asian region and Latin America, as well as Europe and the USA. Over the years, this trend spread throughout the department and solidified MECO's reputation for research excellence. MECO also made key appointments of scholars from other countries who played a crucial role in enlarging the perspectives of the department.

The department's researchers have published leading monographs and edited volumes, some with a signature emphasis on the need for greater internationalisation in the field – for example, Goggin's own *Routledge companion to*

18 Going global

Figure 18.1 Richard Broinowski, Robin Moffat, Steven Maras and long time Australian Embassy liaison Jinny Lee at YTN 24 hour news channel. Seoul, South Korea, 2010. Our host, Ho-Seong Kim was general manager of the station and a graduate of the Master of Media Practice 2006. The visit was organised by Robin to consolidate overseas partnerships. Photo courtesy of Steven Maras

global internet histories (2018). Goggin also established the Digital Rights and Governance in Australia and Asia research group, and has been a globally leading scholar in mobile media and disability media.[1] He is the secretary general of the International Association for Media and Communication Research (IAMCR) based in Prague.

---

1 See more at https://web.archive.org/web/20181226202809/http://digitalrightsusyd.net/.

A very long list of academics have contributed to MECO's internationalisation – below is a brief history of some of the key figures and their work.

The author of *Fresh milk: The secret life of breasts* (2003), Fiona Giles co-edited a special issue of the *International Breastfeeding Journal* on breastfeeding in public. Giles also collaborated as co-editor with Bunty Avieson and Sue Joseph, producing two edited collections for Routledge with international contributors: *Still here: Memoirs of trauma, illness and loss* (2019) and *Mediating memory: Tracing the limits of memoir* (2018).

"That is happening all the time as many edited collections will seek to bring together scholars from a diverse range of countries. It not only showcases work from around the globe, but also extends the relevance of the collection to a broader audience," Giles said.

Alana Mann emerged as a global activist in food politics with her research on La Via Campesina, an organisation that works with farmers from Mexico and Chile on peasant and farmers' rights and food sovereignty. In 2021, Mann was co-chief investigator for FoodLab Sydney, a central element of the City of Sydney's engagement in the Milan Urban Food Policy Pact (MUFPP).

Several academics joined MECO in 2008, bringing with them extensive international expertise. Penny O'Donnell's rich background in international media is evident in her teaching and development of MECO units. A senior lecturer in international media and journalism, she took over as unit coordinator of MECO6926: International Media Practice. O'Donnell has also pursued international research, investigating employment trends and job loss in journalism around the world. The book *Journalists and job loss*, edited by Timothy Marjoribanks, Lawrie Zion, O'Donnell and Merryn Sherwood, was published in 2021.

Stephanie Hemelryk Donald was professor of Chinese Media Studies at MECO in 2009 and 2010. Working across Chinese Studies (with Jeff Riegel) and the School of Literature, Arts and Media, she was part of a major push toward internationalisation at the time.

Fiona Martin's interest in international debates on online media and communications regulation led to research funded by the Australian Research Council (ARC) on safe, inclusive news commenting, with Goggin on global mobile media, and with Tim Dwyer on social media news sharing. Martin and Dwyer co-authored *Sharing news online* (Palgrave, 2019), which examines how the rise of social media platforms has transformed journalism. Martin subsequently won, with colleagues from the University of Sydney and University of Queensland, one of Facebook's first Content Policy on Social Media Awards, producing the report *Facebook: Regulating hate speech in the Asia Pacific* (2021). Martin and Terry Flew also co-edited the open access collection *Digital platform regulation: Global perspectives on internet governance* (2022), and wrote and co-edited, with Gregory Lowe, the RIPE Association for Public Media Researchers' highest selling reader: *The value of public service media* (2014). She has most recently been the Asia region lead on a UNESCO project investigating digital violence against women journalists.

Dwyer became a visiting foreign professor at the College of Media and International Culture, Zhejiang University in 2020. In 2021, Dwyer worked with Jianguo Deng (Fudan University), Yun Wu (Zhejiang University) and Jonathon

Figure 18.2 Tim Dwyer, 2016, photo courtesy of the University of Sydney

Hutchinson (University of Sydney) as part of an international four-year ARC-funded Discovery project exploring innovation and shifts in media pluralism, policies and regulation, researching online news and diversity in China.

Joyce Nip works extensively in the international space. Having worked in television, radio, newspapers and magazines, mainly in Hong Kong, Nip has more than 20 years of experience in journalism teaching, research and practice. She has taught units at graduate and postgraduate level on the processes of media production and consumption in the greater China region.

18 Going global

Much of Nip's research is in political communication and many of her research collaborations have been in Taiwan and Hong Kong. "At the moment I'm working on an externally funded collaborative research project on China's propaganda with a colleague in the School of Languages and Cultures and another colleague in Taiwan, which is supported by an external research grant," she said.

Having worked and taught in multiple countries, Olaf Werder maintains relationships with global partners, among them the University of Nottingham UK; the University of Augsburg, Germany; Fudan University, China; the University of Waikato, Aotearoa New Zealand; and the University of Florida, USA. He has given keynote addresses at many of these institutions. Werder also joined the International Health Humanities Network, where he is an advisory board member working to advance the field in Australia.

Benedetta Brevini's international collaborations have been long-term commitments of two or three years. Three of her book projects involved 50 scholars from around the world. "You have the duty to engage with other scholars that do not belong to your field so you can bring other perspectives. That's particularly true with edited collections, calling on international scholars with particular expertise and publishing with international publishers," she explained.

Brevini holds Visiting Fellowships at the Centre for Law, Justice and Journalism at City University, London; at WZB Berlin Social Science Institute; and at the Centre for Media, Data and Society at the Central European University, Budapest. Of the experience, Brevini said, "Visiting other universities as a researcher and establishing links with like-minded researchers is another pathway to establish fruitful collaborations."

Bunty Avieson continued the work she began in her PhD, investigating the evolving mediascape of the small Himalayan country of Bhutan and how this oral culture has embraced digital media. In 2020, she began an ARC-funded project working with the Bhutanese community in Canberra and Bhutan to contribute to English Wikipedia and to develop their own Dzongkha Wikipedia.

In 2019, Avieson successfully nominated Bhutan's first journalist, Dasho Kinley Dorji, for a University of Sydney Honorary Doctorate. During his visit, Dasho Kinley headlined a special Sydney Ideas event, where he was interviewed by his former classmate, TV compere Andrew Denton, about his extraordinary career, which started when the King of Bhutan sent him to Australia to study journalism in the 1970s.[2]

In July 2020, Avieson was appointed to the Wikimedia Affiliations Committee and Wikimedia Australia. She is chief investigator on a collaboration with the Tata Institute of Social Science in Mumbai, India, along with two colleagues from History at the University of Sydney, in a project that aims to equip members of the Tamil diaspora in Sydney and Mumbai to edit Tamil Wikipedia.

The University of Sydney has established links with universities around the world, including a MECO-specific exchange agreement that Avieson helped secure with O.P. Jindal Global University (JGU) in 2020. Super Exchange Agreements also exist between MECO and the University of Toronto, the University of Copenhagen, the University of Edinburgh, and the University of Texas at Austin.

---

2 Read more at https://www.sydney.edu.au/engage/events-sponsorships/sydney-ideas/2019/dasho-kinley-dorji-and-andrew-denton.html.

18 Going global

The focus on digital cultures, both globally and in the department, has been increasing rapidly. Goggin pointed to this trend, observing that in its second decade, MECO explicitly sought to raise its international profile in the emerging area of digital media studies.

Among the many examples is Hutchinson's collaboration with the University of Hong Kong on "*Blocked by YouTube:* Unseen digital intermediaries for social imaginaries in Vietnam", which was funded through Sydney Southeast Asia Centre (SSEAC).

Justine Humphry has initiated several international collaborations that extend her research on mobile media and marginalised publics. Humphry's multidisciplinary collaboration with the University of Glasgow on the Smart Publics research project examined the social significance, design and governance of smart street furniture. Humphry and Chris Chesher collaborated with Australian and Korean experts to share knowledge of the deployment of robots and smart technologies in public spaces in the Australia–Korea Partnership on Mobile Robot Development in Public Space, led by Naoko Abe in the Sydney Institute for Robotics and Intelligent Systems.

Humphry and Chesher have also been collaborating with Arisa Ema at the University of Tokyo for the Australia/Japan Foundation on Smart Cities in Japan. They plan to run a Smart Cities Forum in Japan, which will draw together researchers, industry and the public at an international event on urban robots, artificial intelligence and the future city.

Olga Boichak is originally from Ukraine, where she managed political campaigns and ran a survey research centre for more than 10 years before joining academia. She was awarded a Fulbright Fellowship in 2014, following the revolution and the ensuing war with Russia, to study the role of digital media in armed conflicts and is now editor of the *Digital War* journal.

Ukraine is the focus of Boichak's two collaborative projects: with Tanya Lokot (Dublin City University), investigating transnational mobilisation in Ukraine's Euromaidan protests; and with Brian McKernan (the Centre for Computational and Data Sciences at Syracuse University, USA), exploring the role of narratives in practices of critical citizenship in Ukraine.

Boichak has organised panels on digital cultures in the Ukrainian context at premier international conferences, such as the International Studies Association Annual Convention, International Communication Association Conference, the Australian Sociological Association and Migrant Belongings. These panels brought together international scholars working at the intersection of media, conflict and activism in the contemporary Ukrainian context. In Sydney, Boichak has continued to work with her long-time mentor, Jeff Hemsley (Syracuse University), with whom she co-led a project on orchestrated interventions and bots in political discourse during elections. In this project, the team developed a novel analytic approach to identify computational propaganda on Twitter and presented their research at the Alan Turing Institute in London.

The collaborations presented above touch only briefly on the various methods academics use to collaborate with colleagues globally. Conferences offer another fertile ground for establishing international collaborations, including those held in Sydney. These have provided vital opportunities for

18 Going global

the exchange of ideas that might lead to research or teaching collaborations.

MECO has hosted numerous international conferences in recent years, including the RIPE 2012 conference of international public service media scholars – the first time this event had been held outside Europe. Goggin recalls the 2017 Australian and New Zealand Communication Association (ANZCA) conference, which showcased the sea change in both national and international scholarship in the field. The conference hosted keynotes from the then International Communication Association president, Paula Gardner (McMaster University); the theorist of global media and communications, Daya Thussu (University of Westminster, then Hong Kong Baptist University); editor of the *Journal of Communication* Silvo Waisbord (George Washington University); and pre-eminent Australian scholar of Chinese media, Wanning Sun (University of Technology Sydney). Other examples include the Crossroads Cultural Studies conference in 2018 and the Journalism Studies Conference in 2019.

Smaller seminar events aimed at kick-starting collaborative research are also frequent. For example, the Health Humanities Conference in 2015, with key scholars from the UK and Shanghai, China, encouraged new approaches to public health communication research. Speakers included Ian Maxwell (University of Sydney), and Hui-Jing Shi (Maternal, Child and Adolescent Health, Fudan University).

The MECO Media@Sydney seminar series, which started in 2007, also has become a destination for international researchers, hosting many leading scholars such as Susanna Paasonen (University of Turku, Finland) and Mark Deuze (University of Amsterdam).

Masterclasses with visiting international scholars and journalists have provided further opportunities for students. A notable example was a masterclass held by David Cay Johnston, a Pulitzer Prize winning investigative journalist and the author of *The making of Donald Trump* (2016).

Giles was also among those who took the opportunity for a teaching exchange and went to Beijing Foreign Studies University. "We organised conferences together and students would then come from Beijing and do a master's, and the same for Fudan, so those are partnerships that were really developed in the course of years," she said.

Goggin recalled, "Various MECO staff taught at overseas universities at various times, such as Steven Maras who took advantage of USYD's longstanding relationship with Fudan University in Shanghai to teach a semester there."

The increasing premium MECO researchers put on fully engaging with the international field is also evident from their participation in key scholarly associations. These include: the International Association for Media and Communication Research (IAMCR); the International Communication Association (of which Flew served as president); the Association of Internet Researchers (with the leadership of Hutchinson); and the World Journalism Education Council (with whom Martin has just finished a global survey of educator attitudes).

Beate Josephi, who retired from Edith Cowan University in 2013, is now an honorary associate working with MECO. She brought many connections with her, including the IAMCR with which she has been involved for more than 20 years, as chair of their journalism research and education section for six years, then as treasurer and chair of the Council's election committee. "It has made me talk to people like Gerard

18 Going global

[Goggin] who is general secretary of IAMCR now for the second time, and I'm very glad about that," she said. "And I was extremely glad to see Fiona Martin elected to the Council."

Among her international endeavours, Josephi lists a stint as visiting professor in 2020 at Suleyman Demirel University (SDU), Almaty, Kazakhstan. This will be an ongoing relationship. Her other work is with the research project Worlds of Journalism Study (WJS) from Ludwig Maximilian University of Munich. The first WJS survey included 21 countries, the second 67 countries, and work has begun on WJS wave3, which includes more than 100 countries. "As part of the WJS team, I'll investigate Uzbekistan with a colleague from SDU for WJS wave3 (for wave2 I did Bhutan). Bunty Avieson is doing Bhutan wave3."

In her view, Australia benefits from being among the most advanced research countries in the English-speaking world. At the same time, she says, "it becomes ever clearer you cannot ignore the rest of the world", citing the increasing tensions between China and the United States as examples of how quickly things can change. "I think it is almost inevitable that you take into consideration all continents, rather than just a few who can speak to each other on more or less equal terms."

Josephi echoes Goggin's view that MECO is well positioned in its international partnerships, especially because of the very high standing of its research, which she says makes the department "enormously attractive" to others as a research partner.

"MECO should continue collaborations not only with the top 50 universities but also with some of those in other countries – especially where students come from – to keep fostering understanding of the world out there. That makes it easy for them and attractive for students to be a student at MECO."

19
How to survive a pandemic
Rebecca Bowman and Victoria Wills

The year 2020 was anything but predictable. We began it choking on the thick haze, terror and disenchantment produced by one of the worst bushfire seasons on record. Nobody could have imagined that once the smoke began to clear, an even deadlier foe would appear on the horizon: a virus, equally as intent on squeezing the air from our lungs.

Margaret Van Heekeren was at home on the evening of Sunday 15 March when an email from the then vice-chancellor and principal, Michael Spence, arrived in her inbox declaring the first confirmed case of COVID-19 on campus. Despite all our precautions, hopes and wishes, it seemed that the virus had finally begun its mutation from international news story to something far closer to home.

"It was like a bomb had gone off. We all scattered and made sure that we were all safe, that we could function," Van Heekeren said.

Her memory of that turning point brought back to life the uncertainty that we all experienced in early 2020. We watched as international flights were cancelled without warning.

Deadlines were set for Australians to return home from overseas. The health crisis began to dominate headlines as analysts attempted to calculate the impact on our economy. From every screen and front page, depictions of the virus, barbed, red and ominous, served as a constant reminder of how deadly this thing could be. We watched and waited.

As infection rates in Australia began to rise, it became apparent that teaching would be affected. In early March, Van Heekeren was the course coordinator in charge of MECO1001: Introduction to Media Studies, a core first year unit with an enrolment of 400 students. Speaking of how MECO responded to national headlines, she remembered it as an interesting atmosphere: "We knew it was coming … we weren't sure when or how we'd go into lockdown … it was such an uncertain time."

The first few weeks of the new semester had already begun, albeit with the usual start-of-semester rollout disrupted due to delays in getting international students safely into the country and onto campus. She described the initial "juggle" required to deliver courses face-to-face, as well as learning how to record lectures so students who were trapped overseas did not miss out. Initially, she said, "that wasn't too much of an issue".

On 15 March, the same day that Spence confirmed the first on-campus COVID-19 case, the NSW government ordered the immediate cancellation of major events with more than 500 people. Three days later, further government restrictions were announced, including a ban on indoor gatherings of over 100 people. No longer able to safely deliver on-campus classes, the vice-chancellor announced that face-to-face teaching would be suspended, with all learning moved online by Monday 23 March. The reality of the new situation quickly became apparent.

19 How to survive a pandemic

Van Heekeren told us: "It was crazy. The beginning of semester is already a really hectic time, and there wasn't time for us to regroup. We just needed to get these students taught in whatever way we could."

By now, we are used to hearing the phrase "the new normal", but Van Heekeren said that during the first lockdown, nothing ever felt "normal". Nor did she feel "comfortable". It was only once everyone "felt secure" that conversations between the teaching staff began. Even that was strange; where previously everyone could simply stop to chat and compare notes in the corridor, now those conversations could only happen online. "We just made contact any way we could," she told us.

Fiona Martin was working as a faculty academic advisor when sudden restrictions were placed on international arrivals into Australia in February, just as many students were due to arrive in Sydney for the start of semester. She was in direct contact with students from the beginning of the lockdown period, carrying out hundreds of pastoral care consultations and advising students across the faculty on how to manage their study progression. It was a deeply worrying time for everyone, particularly for international students who were scattered across the globe, trying to make their way to Australia before the gates slammed shut. Some were paying rent on unoccupied flats in Sydney while they waited to see if they could enter the country.

Martin remembered that one of the biggest hurdles in the beginning was establishing everybody's location. Many students were travelling from China, which faced the toughest restrictions, meaning direct flights were cancelled. These students had to resort to unusual travel routes: "Some of them went to Abu Dhabi. Others went to Thailand or Malaysia.

They were going to intermediary third countries to try to get here."

Martin told us about the extraordinary time it took to work out the whereabouts of each student. Lecturers sent out surveys to collect information about where students were located, as well as what their online access was like. They then cross-referenced this information with their enrolment lists to make sure everybody was accounted for.

Additionally, Martin was concerned about a large cohort of international students who had arrived in Australia for pre-semester language training. When the lockdowns began, those students found themselves stuck in Sydney, with mounting financial pressure and no support network. They reported feeling isolated, depressed and stranded. Undergraduates and postgraduates alike were prevented from socialising or enjoying the campus lifestyle that had drawn them here in the first place.

Yue (Lynette) Mao had just finished her undergraduate studies in Brisbane and was due to travel to Sydney to begin her Master of Media Practice when the lockdown began. Originally from Nianging in Southern China, Mao intended to travel home for the end of year celebrations, but because the virus had already been identified in China she chose to stay and work in Brisbane over the holiday period instead. That meant that by the time Australia's first lockdown had been announced, Mao had not seen her family for over 18 months. She told us: "My mother cried a lot because she really wanted me to go back to China ... I really wanted to go back because I could see her anxiety. She felt so nervous. She was so worried about my safety, my wellbeing."

The 23-year-old was placed in the unenviable position of being separated from all her loved ones overseas, while having no friends or close contacts left in Australia. She knew that if she left the country to travel home even temporarily, she would struggle to return, which would impact her studies.

"I really needed to rely on myself," she said. "I went through a really dark time. I saw the breaking news every day. In that period, I cried a lot."

Mao eventually found a new roommate and together they adopted a kitten, which she says helped them both to get through lockdown. Technology was another lifeline; being able to video call her family every day to report on what they were all eating and where supplies were coming from was a real help.

Times were hard. Yet despite the sudden upheaval, the mounting sense of panic and the urgency of the situation, the department's attention was firmly focused on the wellbeing of its students, often at great personal cost to the staff. Martin said: "We didn't sleep, and weekends disappeared. No one had weekends. We worked weekends. We worked days. We worked nights ... it was tough."

It didn't take long before an action plan for delivering all Semester 1 classes online had been put in place. Martin attributes that speed to the fact that staff within the department are intrinsically "tech savvy". She remembers "a really strong group response with lots of collegial support".

The Faculty of Arts and Social Sciences put together an educational innovation team and created a new program, Online by Our Design. This ensured that all the best teaching strategies were assessed, collated and then published, so that everyone in the faculty had access to the most current and effective teaching protocols. MECO staff were prominent in the faculty response to the changing environment. Following Online by Our Design guidelines, departmental teaching strategies were immediately re-evaluated, alongside an assessment of student enrolments, to establish a pathway through lockdown and beyond. Once it was established how many students intended to continue their studies and how many were located overseas, the task of identifying the correct mix of technologies needed to deliver course content quickly began.

Martin said that in some units up to 75 percent of the cohort were international students, with the majority situated on mainland China. This presented its own set of challenges. It wasn't just a case of altering class content to allow for the new teaching modality, which was time-consuming in itself, but technology proved to be an ongoing complication for offshore students and the department. The most significant problems were caused by China's censorship laws and poor internet access in regional areas, which meant that students often had difficulty accessing University materials online.

Thankfully, this challenge was solved by the Information Technology department, which swiftly acquired additional server space in China to set up a Virtual Private Network (VPN) on behalf of the University. This welcome development was critical to course delivery, enabling students to access course materials outside the Great Firewall of China – a phrase coined by former Australian National University academic Geremie Barmé in his book of the same name, referring to the Chinese Communist Party's policy of internet censorship, blocking access to some foreign websites within its borders.[1] Without the additional server capacity and VPN, it would have been impossible for thousands of students in mainland China to continue their studies.

---

1 Griffiths, 2021.

19 How to survive a pandemic

Within two weeks of the border closures and restrictions being instituted within New South Wales, MECO was able to offer a fully functioning online education environment for domestic and international students, with all tutorials hosted on Zoom. The department also relied on other online tools to deliver the student experience. Martin remembers, "We used so many different platforms aside from the Canvas suite. People would be using Instagram, Facebook, Twitter, Padlet, Socratic, Miro, YouTube, Vimeo and SoundCloud. We used every available online technology."

As far as memories of 2020 go, the now ubiquitous video conferencing platform Zoom would likely top the list for many. Learning how to use the platform was a baptism of fire for most, with the majority developing a love–hate relationship. With the extra barriers of the unmute button, audio lag and unreliable microphones, in-class discussion (especially small breakout group work) was less likely than when sharing a physical space.

Asked how she felt about online lessons, Mao responded: "I can understand why my Chinese friends didn't turn on the video ... because often they just [woke] up ... If I can't see anyone, I choose to be silent. I don't know why ... It's just so weird to talk to the camera."

Between technology issues and student reluctance to switch on their webcams, it became impossible for educators to "read the room" and spot which students were struggling. It also highlighted the educational differences between Socratic teaching practices used in Australia, which encourage open dialogue and critical thinking, and the Chinese Confucian method, which is more concerned with listening than discussion-based education. This new atmosphere was not what was expected by many local students, used to vigorous classroom debates, but many positives were also noted. For instance, some students who previously felt too shy to speak up in class were happy to take advantage of the text-based chat function in Zoom.

For Sydney-based students, the ability to study from home and avoid time-consuming commutes into campus were widely reported as the greatest benefits. This was also advantageous for many overseas students. As Mao told us, "Some of my friends said it's okay to study in China because they can save the living fee … it's a really good way for those people who just want to finish the degree as soon as possible. They can save more money and they can work. They can have a full-time job and do full-time study."

The department's production-based units were hit particularly hard by COVID-19 restrictions, facing additional challenges and demonstrating the limits to what could be delivered remotely. Staff and students alike had a steep learning curve adapting to online learning, relying on what students had on hand rather than the department's on-campus resources. We personally experienced the difficulties of learning practical, technology-based skills without on-campus resources. Courses teaching hands-on skills had previously run with access to purpose-built studios and classrooms on campus, making use of professional equipment and multiple large screens. For instance, the Digital Media Unit (see Chapter 6) enabled students to gain experience with professional audiovisual equipment, whether using the state-of-the-art recording studio in the Education Building or borrowing portable microphones and sound device kits. Now, most students would be relying on their laptops, toggling between Zoom in one window and programs such as Adobe InDesign and Audition in another.

19 How to survive a pandemic

The Digital Media Unit equipment was central to the undergraduate and postgraduate podcasting units coordinated by Lea Redfern. When first asked if these units could be taught remotely, she initially said no, "because students won't have access to the things we teach". Luckily for students, she reconsidered. MECO2601: Media Production: Radio and Podcasting was a Semester 1 core unit for many undergraduate students. "It would be really terrible for students to have a second-year compulsory subject interrupted in that way," Redfern explained. "So, I really needed to find a way to make it work." She turned to the media industry for inspiration to see how traditional practices were diversifying in response to the crisis.

Redfern found that parts of the industry that relied on audio technology, such as radio and podcasting, were facing the same challenges as the education sector. Professional podcasters and radio journalists had to adapt to work under these unprecedented conditions. The industry response provided something of a blueprint for how students could be taught using the technology they had at hand, with smartphones acting as recording devices and Zoom enabling remote interviews (like the ones conducted for this chapter).

"Things that weren't central to the course, to do with remote recording and making do with what you've got, became central to the course," Redfern says. "That wasn't just happening within our course, it was happening in industry. I started to feel really confident that what we were teaching wasn't just a Mickey Mouse version. This is the version that you will need to know if you're going out into industry as well."

Radio and podcast listeners had also demonstrated they were willing to adapt, with domestic sounds and interruptions becoming an accepted part of the audio space. Redfern says this adaptability is "part of the COVID story too". Embracing this mindset allowed students to "solve problems in a real-world kind of way ... One of the things we tried to emphasise in audio is that all the stuff they were learning has practical applications for the real world, and it will help them no matter where they go with audio."

While remote learning posed significant challenges for students, many performed exceptionally in the new learning environment. Redfern remembers podcasting students who went "all out", adding sound effects to basic exercises designed to assess writing skills, and producing amazing and often very personal audio pieces. In other units and throughout the department, grades went up during the first semester of 2020, with more high marks awarded and fewer students failing units than in previous years. According to Van Heekeren, the reason for this is obvious: "You're at home, you're in lockdown. What are you going to do but study?"

Possibly for related reasons, enrolment rates for 2020's second semester were better than expected. During the turbulent first semester, amid warnings that university enrolments were going down, Redfern remembers checking the numbers for her second semester postgraduate podcasting unit. She was surprised to see 250 students were due to take the course: around 60 more students than the previous year, continuing the year-on-year growth trend for that unit. The situation was similar throughout the department. When the pandemic first took effect, Van Heekeren watched the enrolment numbers for MECO1001: Introduction to Media Studies drop from around 400 students to 299. But the 2021 cohort for the same unit boomed, with 684 students, making it the unit's biggest enrolment ever. Around 500 of these students were studying online from mainland China. The numbers were a promising sign of the health of MECO, at odds with the pessimistic view of the state of the university sector prevalent in national media.

Martin points to the unique problems in ensuring the MECO curriculum could openly and comprehensively cover global media issues when many students were subject to China's controls on political expression. The week her ARIN2610: Internet Transformations lecture was due to explore the Hong Kong protestors' use of digital technologies, many Chinese students didn't attend. One student told her they would not show up because the topic was "too sensitive". Those students, located in China, were possibly concerned about online surveillance in ways they would not be in an on-campus lecture in Australia. Another industry-based unit, FASS4903: ABC Innovation Research Project Unit, could not be delivered in China, because students could not access the ABC's services. Considered alongside student difficulties accessing reliable internet connections, and unwillingness to participate in discussions online, challenges like these make Martin doubtful the department can fully "deliver the level of critical, analytical education that the University of Sydney is known for" to students studying at home from China.

While online has opened up new possibilities, there are many aspects of on-campus learning that can't be replicated in the virtual environment. As time passed, many students and staff seemed eager to return to campus. In September 2020, Redfern organised a Saturday workshop in response to emails from postgraduate podcasting students begging for the opportunity to experience the on-campus facilities. Asked whether MECO's future would be increasingly remote and online, Martin was unconvinced: "We don't want to get rid of the face-to-face experience ... people obviously do value it, and we enjoy it. So, no, we're not going to go and become a distance education provider."

Even so, the success of MECO in adapting its teaching to a COVID-safe context has shown what is possible to achieve remotely. "We will certainly be retaining some online elements in the future," said Van Heekeren.

The ways in which the 2020 experience will shape the department are yet to be seen. Questions remain on whether students will continue to enrol in greater numbers, and whether they will study remotely or on-campus. These outcomes will have ramifications for the balance between domestic and international students, and to what extent new technologies adopted during the pandemic will remain in place as in-person teaching returns.

When we look back on the height of the pandemic years, it is easy to recall the devastating effects of COVID-19: the mainstream story that has been spun of human suffering, financial devastation and fear for the future. There are, however, positives to be found, and the story of MECO is one of them. Like a phoenix rising from the ashes, maybe one day we will come to see the pandemic as a serendipitous turning point, not just for MECO, but for all humanity. As Van Heekeren puts it: "I think when we look back in another decade or so, we will see that 2020 was more like a reset year. Looking back, there is a feeling of satisfaction ... relief that we actually managed to keep this thing afloat. There is something enjoyable about that."

Works cited

Griffiths, J. T. (2021). *The great firewall of China: How to build and control an alternative version of the internet.* https://doi.org/10.5040/9781350257948

20
Digital and post-digital futures for communications: MECO in the 2020s and beyond

Terry Flew

The essays in this collection have critically reflected on the 20-year history of the Department of Media and Communications (MECO) at the University of Sydney. I commenced in MECO in 2021 but have followed the evolution of the program since its commencement in 2000. One of the major transformations in MECO over this 20-year history has been the incorporation of the Digital Cultures program (see Chapter 4), to the point where it is now close to providing the largest suite of programs in the department.

In undertaking this chapter, I note work that I have undertaken previously, reviewing Media and Communications courses in Australia, for a collection of essays dealing with innovation in Australian arts, media and design.[1] In my own contribution to this collection, I observed that the early 2000s saw a rapid growth in media and communications courses, led by the Group of Eight or "sandstone" universities such as

---

1 Wissler et al., 2004.

the University of Sydney and the University of Melbourne.[2] I described this phenomenon as follows:

> From its origins in the newer universities Media and Communications courses have increasingly presented themselves to cash-strapped Arts Deans as a relatively low-cost way to tap into the interests and media literacy of young people, present the *cachet* of vocational orientation, and provide practical skills development and job opportunities at the end of the degree. If academic degrees were traded on some form of stock exchange Media and Communications courses would certainly constitute what market commentators term a "growth stock".[3]

A lot of that description still sounds valid to a description of the MECO programs at the University of Sydney today. Our student numbers are far in excess of most departments in the Faculty of Arts and Social Sciences, the courses have very high international students demand, graduates of the programs are highly sought after in the media and digital industries, and the majors remain highly popular in the generalist BA program as they tap into digital literacies and the preoccupations of young people.

Over a 20-year period, the principal animating changes have come under the banner of "*the digital*". In some respects, this is old news. In the 1990s, scholars associated with the "*multiliteracies*" movement were observing that fields such as media and cultural studies needed to move from critique

---

2   Flew, 2004.
3   Flew, 2004, p. 111.

20 Digital and post-digital futures for communications

to a world where the tools and techniques of digital media production were becoming far more accessible, and to think in terms of design, as students increasingly became content creators.[4] As the creative industries became more prominent worldwide, the divides between both theory and production, and between critical and vocational education, were being broken up by movements as varied as the maker movement, DIY online innovation, and creator cultures.[5] Having authored a leading textbook on new media over four editions between 2002 and 2014, I myself had become very much aware by the fourth edition that the claims to being "new" were looking somewhat contentious.[6]

At the same time, the rise of the Digital Cultures major at undergraduate level and the success of the Master of Digital Communication and Culture at a postgraduate level have clearly been MECO success stories in recent years. Its history is accounted for elsewhere in the book, but its uptake after a near-death experience as Arts Informatics (see Chapter 4) has been nothing short of remarkable. Digital Cultures has tapped into the shift towards the digital creative economy, where the fastest growing occupations are in fields such as digital marketing, social media, data analytics and user experience design, while traditional communications professions such as journalism, public relations, and the print and publishing industries are static or declining.[7] It has also tapped into the imaginations of international students, particularly those from

---

4 Kellner, 2002; Kress, 1997.
5 Gauntlett, 2011; Hartley, 2012; Wilson, 2002.
6 Flew, 2014.
7 National Skills Commission, 2021.

China, as the Digital China and Internet Plus agendas drive the nation's next phase of economic development.[8]

The programs offered by MECO at the University of Sydney are therefore flourishing, to a degree that exceeds expectations from when they were first established. But could the bubble burst?

There are some warning signs on the horizon. The federal government's Job-Ready Graduates package, which places communications, humanities and social sciences courses in the highest HECS band, was a deliberate piece of social engineering to shift demand away from such courses. It was not backed by any substantive empirical evidence, but it furthers a perception that communication and the arts are not high priority areas in the eyes of policymakers.

International student demand is very much vulnerable to the vicissitudes of Australia–China diplomatic relations. It is not inconceivable that Chinese authorities could further discourage their citizens from enrolling in courses in Australian universities, and the need to diversify international student demand is very apparent. At the same time, MECO courses at the University seem to have benefitted from what Scott Galloway (New York University) has termed the "K-shaped recovery" from the COVID-19 pandemic, where elite programs are experiencing a sharp upturn in demand while many other programs are facing sharp declines in student demand.[9]

A third set of variables arise from the COVID-19 pandemic itself. The public health response to the COVID-19 emergency has changed many things around the world, from travel and

---

8   Hong, 2017; Li, 2019.
9   Galloway, 2021.

20 Digital and post-digital futures for communications

tourism to entertainment and shopping. In higher education, it saw the end of a 25-year debate about the pros and cons of face-to-face versus online education, as 2020 saw every course in every university around the world have to develop a strategy for teaching online.

While this will not remain post-pandemic, there will also not be a return to the pre-2020 educational orthodoxy. Just as workers increasingly expect to be able to work outside of the office, students brought up on Netflix, YouTube and "content anywhere any time" will expect a mix of online and in-person course delivery, with the elements that need to be undertaken on-campus requiring close consideration (marking the end of the 500-seat lecture theatre, to take one example). The University of Sydney is not traditionally an online university, so there is considerable retooling to be done in order to be active in this space. Moreover, insofar as going online makes our courses available throughout the world, it also makes everyone else's course available to prospective students. The University's future competitors may be less UNSW, UTS and Macquarie University, and more the London School of Economics, Goldsmiths and the Annenberg Schools of the University of Pennsylvania and the University of Southern California.

There is the question of the future of research in MECO. This can be understood both in terms of emergent research fields and the wider research ecosystem. To take the second of these first, we can see that the 2000–20 period saw the emergence and growth of a particular research funding regime in Australia. Its characteristics included:

- The scaling up of arts and humanities research around Centres of Excellence and Cooperative Research Centres

etc., alongside new strategies to tap into sources of funding outside of the Australian Research Council (ARC), such as the corporate sector and federal, state and local government agencies.
- A consistent reduction in the direct funding of research by the federal government, creating a research funding "gap", accentuated by the need to have a standing reserve of research capacity through centres that could offer rolling contracts to researchers able to attract research income, particularly from non-ARC sources.[10]
- The development of research ranking systems such as Excellence in Research for Australia (ERA) with elaborate performance metrics dashboards to rank universities as "world-class" or above across multiple disciplines.
- The massive recruitment of international fee-paying students, with the largest number coming from China, who enrolled in degrees such as business, engineering, information technology and, notably and perhaps surprisingly, media and communications.

The year 2020 saw this edifice shudder, if not completely collapse. The onset of COVID-19 saw international student enrolments stall at most universities, as travel to Australia was no longer possible. Even placing COVID-19 aside, deteriorating Australia–China diplomatic relations, combined with a backlash towards the Chinese government and economic dependency on China in Australia, mean that there

---

10 At my former place of employment, the Creative Industries Faculty at the Queensland University of Technology, the number of research-only positions at one point constituted one quarter of the faculty and had claims to being a school in its own right. Indeed, t-shirts were made up to represent the Research Intensive Group (RIG), and I still have one in my wardrobe.

is no going back to primarily funding research through international student enrolments.[11]

The commitment to scaling up research remains, as does the focus on research income from non-ARC sources. But the commitment to research-only staff funded through lavish research centres and institutes is being viewed very carefully, and most of those now employed in universities are expected to teach as well as research. Also, with no additional funding tied to ERA outcomes, the exercise has come to resemble a large and lavish beauty pageant, albeit one where the prizes resemble those awarded on ABC shows such as *Hard Quiz* rather than the bounteous funding once promised when the scheme was first announced in the late 2000s. There is no evidence that ERA outcomes influence student enrolment decisions in any tangible manner, other than possibly inducing greater confidence in staff in a well-ranked school or department (and fear in lower-ranked ones).[12]

MECO could be well placed in the emerging environment. The connections of academic staff to other parts of the University are well developed, ranging from law, economics and the social sciences, to architecture, design and planning, to information technology, agriculture and the health sciences. As new, large-scale multidisciplinary teams are developing, it can be expected that academics from MECO will be a pivotal part of this.

Through both the Digital Cultures program, and the "digital turn" within MECO, there is capacity to be at the

---

11 Brophy, 2021.
12 In 2022 the newly elected Albanese Labor Government chose to abolish the ERA. At time of publication (2024) it had not been replaced by another research ranking exercise.

forefront of the emergent trends in communications and media globally. From my experience in the International Communications Association (ICA) – of which I was the president from 2019 to 2020 – I would observe that these growth areas are:

- Human–machine (post-digital) communication and automated decision-making (machine–machine communication).
- Computational methods for social research drawing upon large-scale data analytics.
- Activism and social justice concerns in media representation, media and creative industries, and digital communication.
- The platformisation of cultural production, and how media industry studies is being both "platformised" and transformed by the growing reliance upon content distribution through digital platforms.
- The intersection between post-globalisation and the "techlash" around the power of digital platforms, leading to renewed focus on nation-state regulation of digital platforms and online content.[13]

MECO already has a strong base in all these areas. Going into the 2020s, the discipline is in a new School of Art, Communication and English more closely aligned to the Sydney College of the Arts, and to be branded as a school where our students and staff are "making culture", particularly with digital technologies. This is where the Digital Cultures major, and much of MECO more generally, has been, but its previous home in a diffuse School of Literature, Art and Media (SLAM) lacked both internal logic and external profile. Mapping this innovative teaching profile to our leading-edge

---

13   Flew, 2018.

research in digital and post-digital media points to an exciting future for the department, its staff, its programs and its students.

Works cited

Brophy, D. (2021). *China panic: Australia's alternative to paranoia and pandering*. Black Ink Books.

Flew, T. (2004). Media and communication. In R. Wissler, B. Haseman, S. Wallace & M. Keane (Eds.), *Innovation in Australian arts, media and design* (pp. 111–22). Post Pressed.

Flew, T. (2014). *New media: An introduction* (4th ed.). Oxford University Press.

Flew, T. (2018). Post-globalisation. *Javnost – The Public*, 25(1–2), 102–109. https://doi.org/10.1080/13183222.2018.1418958.

Galloway, S. (2021, April 30). *Higher Ed 2.0: What we got right/wrong*. No Mercy/No Malice. https://www.profgalloway.com/higher-ed-2-0-what-we-got-right-wrong/

Gauntlett, D. (2011). *Making is connecting*. Polity.

Hartley, J. (2012). *Digital futures for cultural and media studies*. Wiley-Blackwell. https://doi.org/10.4324/9780203814284.

Hong, Y. (2017). *Networking China: the digital transformation of the Chinese economy*. University of Illinois Press. https://doi.org/10.5406/illinois/9780252040917.001.0001.

Kellner, D. (2002). New media and new literacies: Reconstructing education for the new millennium. In *Handbook of new media* (pp. 90–104). SAGE. https://doi.org/10.4135/9781446206904.n8.

Kress, G. (1997). Visual and verbal modes of representation in electronically mediated communication: The potentials of new forms of text. In I. Snyder (Ed.), *Page to screen: Taking literacy into the electronic era* (pp. 53–79). Allen & Unwin. https://doi.org/10.4324/9780203201220_chapter_3.

Li, L. (2019). *Zoning China: Online video, popular culture, and the state*. MIT Press. https://doi.org/10.7551/mitpress/11675.001.0001.

National Skills Commission. (2021). *Labour market insights*. https://www.nationalskillscommission.gov.au/

Wilson, H. (2002). Towards a non-binary approach to communication. *Media International Australia, 28*(2), 1–18. https://doi.org/10.1177/1329878X0210500101.

Wissler, R., Haseman, B., Wallace, S., & Keane, M. (2004). *Innovation in Australian arts, media and design.* Post Pressed.

MECO timeline

1999	Catharine Lumby starts work on designing the UG degree; office in RC Mills
2000	Media & Communications UG degree introduced
2001	Anne Dunn joins; MECO computer lab created; Brennan Building 215 refurbished for MECO; Richard Broinowski becomes adjunct professor in Media Studies
2002	First technical officer appointed, employed by school reporting to Chair of MECO (Adrian Langker)
2003	Kate Crawford joins MECO; first internship officer appointed; staff offices move to basement level of RC Mills
2004	Chris Chesher joins (to direct Arts Informatics degree, not yet part of MECO); Marc Brennan and Richard Stanton join MECO; honours degree introduced; Master of Media Practice introduced; Overseas Fellowship Program established; tech officers supporting MECO

assigned from META Centre in the faculty; first equipment booking software installed, procured from UTS – ermplanet

2005 Steven Maras, Megan Le Masurier and Fiona Giles join MECO; TV Studio created in the Education Building; Education Building 209, 210, 211, 212 – MOU with Education – refurbished

2006 Gerard Goggin joins MECO; MECO becomes a department; third tech officer position created to cater for television studio (Daragh Lane); Arts Hub for Online Media – AHOME – built in the Transient Building, rooms 170 and 171 created in the Transient Building from the former META Centre labs; Master of Strategic Public Relations introduced; Master of Digital Communication and Culture introduced (not yet part of MECO); Robin Moffat joins MECO as internship coordinator (until May 2014)

2007 Catharine Lumby leaves for UNSW, Gerard and Kate Crawford join her; Alana Mann and Sean Chaidaroon join MECO; Master of Publishing introduced

2008 Fiona Martin, Penny O'Donnell, Antonio Castillo and Tim Dwyer join MECO; Radio Room acquired, Holme C104 negotiated with University of Sydney Union

2009 MECO staff move to Level 1 and Level 2 Holme Footbridge Terrace refurbished offices (first time all staff together – previously in Mills and Woolley Buildings); Steven Maras chair; Sean Chaidaroon leaves; Stephanie Donald joins as professor of Chinese Media Studies, then honorary professor of Media Studies; PG internship coordinator position created (Fran Hagon); Master of Health Communication introduced

MECO timeline

2010 Joyce Nip joins as an inter-school appointment; Faculty Arts Digital disbanded, MECO to provide own tech support; Alison Ray joins MECO; Radio Room refurbished, Holme C104 security upgrade; Peter Fray from *The Sydney Morning Herald* appointed as First Decade Fellow December 2010 to April 2011

2011 Goggin re-appointed to MECO as inaugural professor; Olaf Werder joins MECO, Marc Brennan chair; Digital Media Unit created, facilities spread across the University, including loans store in Brennan MacCallum. Digital media manager appointed and digital technology officers audio, video (Phil Glen)

2012 Death of Anne Dunn; Gerard Goggin chair; Marc Brennan and Antonio Castillo leave

2013 Merge between MECO and DC; Benedetta Brevini, Grant Bollmer and Jonathon Hutchinson join MECO

2014 MECO staff joined by Digital Cultures (from Level 3 Woolley) and Digital Media Unit on refurbished Level 2 Woolley; Bunty Avieson joins; Adriana Hernandez starts as an UG internship officer; Richard Broinowski and Richard Stanton leave MECO; Fiona Giles chair (until 2015); Media Lab Brennan LS120 created, Media Lab merges with eLearning spaces

2015 Mitchell Hobbs joins MECO

2016 Tim Dwyer chair

2017 Alana Mann chair; Margaret Van Heekeren, Marcus Carter and Justine Humphry join MECO; Grant Bollmer leaves

2018   Tim Dwyer chair; Francesco Bailo, Diana Chester, Heather Horst, Lea Redfern and Jolynna Sinanan join MECO; podcasting studio built in Education Building (replacing space in Holme Building)

2019   Alana Mann chair; Olga Boichak and Mark Johnson join MECO; VR lab built in the Education Building

2021   Terry Flew joins; Catharine Lumby returns – chair

2022   Alana Mann leaves for the University of Tasmania; new staff: Agata Mrva-Montoya, Catherine Page Jeffery, Joanne Gray, John Hartley, Xiang Reng, Margie Borschke; Gerard Goggin returns; MECO becomes a discipline (August)

About the authors

Nikbanoo Ardalan completed her Bachelor of Arts/Bachelor of Advanced Studies at the University of Sydney. After finishing high school in her home country, Iran, she decided to study film and media in Australia. She is now pursuing a Master of Arts at the Free University of Berlin.

Anna Jenica Bacud has a Bachelor of Arts in Journalism from the University of the Philippines Diliman and has recently completed her Master of Media Practice at the University of Sydney. From being a student media producer to a multimedia officer with the Business Co-Design media team at the University of Sydney Business School, she has led the creation and production of *Work, Live, Play, Learn: Co-Lab*, a podcast series bringing student voices together during times of crisis and uncertainty. She also has extensive experience in content production, having worked in media (TV) and events as a copywriter, promo producer, content strategist and events writer. She aspires to travel the world and share little stories that matter.

Olga Boichak is a senior lecturer in Digital Cultures at the University of Sydney, where she leads the Computational Social Science Lab. She is a media sociologist whose research interests span networks, narratives and cultures of activism surrounding military conflicts. Boichak has written for a range of academic and popular media on the topics of participatory cultures and humanitarianism in Russia's war against Ukraine. Her auto-ethnographic essay, "Hidden bread and hidden histories", has inspired an award-winning Missing Chapter documentary (Vox, 2022). She is a chief investigator on an ARC-funded project that maps topographies of digital sovereignty, as well as a portfolio of other projects that explore the geopolitical implications of digital media.

Rebecca Bowman earned her Master of Media Practice degree from the University of Sydney in 2021 and holds a Bachelor of Laws degree from the University of Hull, UK. As the Communications Manager for the Foyer Foundation, Bowman now dedicates her time to expanding the reach and impact of Youth Foyers across Australia, working towards securing thriving, independent futures for children and young people at risk of or experiencing homelessness. When she is not shaping impactful communication strategies, Bowman enjoys exploring the world with her husband and three sons. For a continuous stream of words and pictures, visit Bowman's Instagram profile at @becs_life_in_boxes, or connect with her on LinkedIn.

Cindy Cameronne studied a Master of Media Practice from 2019 to 2021 at the University of Sydney and has a Bachelor of Laws/Bachelor of Arts from the Australian National University. She now works at legal news start-up *Lawyerly* as the Sydney bureau chief, with prior experience as a senior editor at Thomson Reuters.

Longtong (Sylvie) Chen is a 2021 graduate from the Master of Media Practice at the University of Sydney. She completed her undergraduate degree in English at the Southern Medical University in Guangzhou, China. She is now working as a journalist in a news agency and enjoys using her skills to contribute to exciting news reports, listening to others, proposing questions and translating them into words on the page. She also likes to travel to different places and enjoy local cultures and customs.

Chris Chesher is senior lecturer in Digital Cultures in the discipline of Media and Communications. He has been working at the University of Sydney since 2004. His research concerns the cultural dimensions of digital technologies such as the historical and conceptual development of computers, the everyday spatiality of video games, and the urban contexts of smart street furniture and mobile robots. He teaches the units ARIN6903: Digital Media and Society and ARIN3610: Technology and Culture.

Johanna Ellersdorfer is a writer and paintings conservator. She is currently completing a PhD at the University of Sydney exploring creative writing by contemporary artists and writers, examining experiences of materiality and publishing as a creative and artistic practice. She holds qualifications in art theory, creative writing and cultural materials conservation and has particular interests in technical art history and creative non-fiction. Her academic work has been published in journals including *TEXT* and the *AICCM Bulletin* and her creative work has appeared in the *Australian Multilingual Writing Project* and the *University of Sydney Anthology*. She was shortlisted for the 2020 Deborah Cass Prize and was the 2022 Ross Steele AM Fellow at the State Library of NSW.

Terry Flew is professor of digital communication and culture at the University of Sydney, and an Australian Research Council Laureate Fellow. He is the author of 16 books (six edited), including *The creative industries, culture and policy* (Sage, 2012), *Global creative industries* (Polity, 2013), *Media economics* (Palgrave, 2015), *Understanding global media* (Palgrave, 2018), *Regulating platforms* (Polity, 2021) and *Handbook of the digital media economy* (SAGE, 2022). He was president of the International Communications Association (ICA) from 2019 to 2020 and was an executive board member of the ICA 2017–23. He was elected an ICA Fellow in 2019. He is a Fellow of the Australian Academy of the Humanities (FAHA), elected in 2019. He has held visiting professor roles at City University, London, George Washington University, Communications University of China, and University of Nottingham Ningbo China.

Chris Gillies is a writer from the New South Wales Mid North Coast with a passion for creative non-fiction, landscape and farming. In 2019, he completed a Graduate Certificate in Creative Writing at the University of Sydney. Outside of university he is a published journalist writing about farming for publications in Australia, the USA and the UK. Chris is undertaking a Master of Arts (Research) at the University of Sydney's United States Study Centre specialising in how

About the authors

masculinity shapes the relationship between coach and player. He cannot play sport.

Kiran Gupta is a media and law graduate of the University of Sydney. He is a keen journalist, having published for the *Sydney Morning Herald*, *The Guardian*, *The Daily Telegraph*, *Mamamia*, *Popmatters* and others. In 2023, he was a finalist for Young Journalist of the Year in the Premier's Multicultural Communications Awards. Throughout his degree, he completed exchange studies in International Journalism and Rural Indian journalism through the London School of Economics and Jindal Global University. He also undertook an internship at the *Sydney Morning Herald* where he published over 20 articles. He currently manages and writes for his own independent theatre publication.

Catharine Lumby is a professor of media at the University of Sydney where she was founding Chair of the Media and Communications department. She was also the founding Director of the Journalism and Media Research Centre at UNSW. Prior to entering academia, she worked for two decades as a print and TV journalist for the *Sydney Morning Herald*, the ABC and *The Bulletin* magazine. She has written and co-authored 10 books, and numerous book chapters and journal articles. Her most recent book is *Frank Moorhouse: A Life* (2023).

Agata Mrva-Montoya is a lecturer and degree director of the Master of Publishing at MECO. Previously she worked for over 15 years in scholarly and educational book publishing, commissioning and project-managing a wide range of non-fiction titles, producing ebooks and implementing accessible publishing practices. Her research focuses on innovation, technology and power in the publishing industry. She has published on the impact of digital technologies and new business models on scholarly communication and the book publishing industry in general. She seeks to align her current research projects with her interest and experience with accessibility, design thinking and digital technologies, in the belief that publishing can play an important role in creating a better society.

Cheryl O'Byrne completed her PhD at the University of Sydney in 2023. Her research explores the relationships between aesthetics, ethics and politics in filial life narratives about mothers. Her work has been published in *Australian Literary Studies, a/b: Auto/biography Studies* and *Life Writing*. She is working on a monograph under contract with Routledge.

Penny O'Donnell is senior lecturer in international media and journalism at the University of Sydney. Her current teaching roles include coordination of two postgraduate units of study: MECO6926: International Media Practice (core unit) and MECO6928: Media and Communication Internship (capstone unit). Her current research explores two important issues in international media and journalism: first, addressing journalism's vulnerabilities in the era of generative artificial intelligence, by exploring the news/information skills and capabilities that smart machines may have trouble replicating. Second, addressing the rise of non-democratic rivals to Western transnational media networks, by critically analysing contraflows designed to counter the prevailing narratives of international news coverage. In 2023, O'Donnell was appointed to the role of vice-president (research) for the Journalism Education and Research Association of Australia (JERAA). Most recently, in partnership with Ayesha Jehangir, she co-convened the ECR/HDR Day for the JERAA 2023 Conference hosted by UTS.

Tim Piccione graduated from the University of Sydney in 2020, completing a Master of Media Practice in the Media and Communications department. He also previously completed a Bachelor of Political, Economic and Social Sciences at the university in 2016. During his postgraduate studies, Tim was awarded the Anne Dunn Memorial Prize for Outstanding Performance in both Podcasting and Media Writing, and contributed to *The Junction* journalism project. He remained involved with MECO after graduating, tutoring first year undergraduate Media Studies students under Margaret Van Heekeren. He now lives in the ACT, working as a court reporter for *The Canberra Times*. He previously wrote for *The Daily Advertiser* in Wagga as a local reporter and for national publications *Urban List* and *Broadsheet*.

Alexandra Spence is a sound-artist and musician living on unceded Wangal Land in Sydney. Through her practice Spence reimagines the intricate relationships between the listener, the object, and the surrounding environment as a kind of communion or conversation. Her aesthetic favours field recordings, analogue technologies and object interventions. Spence has presented her work globally including BBC Radio; Café Oto, London; Elektronmusikstudion, Stockholm; Museo Reina Sofia, Madrid; Radiophrenia Festival, Glasgow; Sound Forms Festival, Hong Kong; Vancouver Art Gallery; &

Liveworks Festival, Liquid Architecture, Carriageworks; Phoenix Central Park; &Volume Festival, AGNSW, Sydney. She's received grants from the Australia Council, CreateNSW, APRA AMCOS, and has released her music with Room40, Longform Editions, and Mappa. Spence completed a Master of Fine Arts in sound installation at Simon Fraser University, Vancouver, and works as a technical officer for the Digital Media Unit and a casual academic at the University of Sydney. Find her at alexandraspence.net.

Marco Stojanovik completed a Graduate Certificate in Media Practice at the University of Sydney in 2020, focusing on journalism and media theory units, having previously graduated with a Bachelor of International and Global Studies. During his studies, he took part in a communications internship at the International Federation of Journalists Asia-Pacific and volunteered at other advocacy organisations concerning media freedom and digital rights, among other issues. His feature articles have been published in *The Junction*, *Salience* and *Megaphone OZ*, and his opinion pieces, essays and news reviews on the websites of the Organization for World Peace, Seven Pillars Institute for Global Finance and Ethics, and the German-Southeast Asian Center of Excellence for Public Policy and Good Governance. He also writes history and tourism-based web content and teaches English as a second language. In his spare time, he likes to visit and write about Sydney's beaches for his blog *Every Sydney Beach*.

Weien Su has a Master of Media Practice (2021) from the University of Sydney and a Bachelor of Media in Public Relations and Advertising (2020) from the University of New

South Wales. During her studies, she participated in a range of university activities including a postgraduate student leader program and virtual student peer program, and led the Chinese Student Association in the department. Outside university, she worked for two years in a local advertising agency as a part-time account executive and content writer. In 2021, she moved back to China to pursue her passion in advertising.

Pam Walker joined MECO in 2008 as a casual lecturer. She has taught and coordinated MECO6900: News Writing, MECO6901: Dealing with the Media and MECO1001: Introduction to Media Studies. Walker is currently editorial director and editor-in-chief of *Salience,* which publishes outstanding student work, and the University of Sydney campus editor for *The Junction,* a website that showcases student journalism from 27 universities across Australia and the Pacific region. She has also taught news and feature writing, media law, and investigative journalism at UTS, Western Sydney University and UNSW. Walker has worked as a journalist and editor for more than 25 years and was press secretary for Lord Mayor of Sydney Clover Moore.

Jenny Welsh currently works as a freelance editor and proofreader. After being employed for many years in the IT industry, she decided to embark on a career change and study a Master of Publishing at the University of Sydney. She has been studying and working part time for the past three years. She graduated with an honours degree in languages from the University of the West of England in the UK and spent several years living and working in the Netherlands before eventually emigrating to Australia. When she is not working, Welsh loves to spend time with her family on the coast, and to push herself to master new and more challenging yoga poses.

Olaf Werder holds a senior lectureship in the Faculty of Arts and Social Sciences at the University of Sydney. After a professional career in the communication industry, working for broadcast media sales and advertising agencies, he held academic appointments at the University of Florida and the University of New Mexico in the United States prior to joining the University of Sydney in 2011. As the program director for health communication, he is responsible for all core units in the degree program each year, which are typically offered in multiple in-person seminars. In general, his research focuses on investigating how people communicate and understand health to identify community-collaborative pathways for system changes and improved health outcomes. Working with colleagues in Australia and abroad, he explores issues of health equity, health humanities and social practice approaches and how they relate to communication practice.

Victoria Wills is a Master of Publishing graduate and currently works at NewSouth Books. She lived in London for four years, working in the arts, before returning to her hometown of Sydney in 2020. Before that, she completed a Bachelor of International and Global Studies in 2016, also at the University of Sydney. Her postgraduate studies have been greatly affected by COVID-19, and the contrast between her experiences studying on campus and studying online greatly inspired her work on the pandemic chapter in this volume, cowritten with Rebecca Bowman. In her spare time, she writes short stories and other things, reads widely, bushwalks, sews and swims.

About the authors

Yonglin (Tina) Zhu has a Bachelor of Insurance and Accounting (2020) from the Southwestern University of Finance and Economics and is now taking postgraduate courses in Media Practice at the University of Sydney. During her undergraduate studies, she participated in a wide range of campus activities. She once served as reporter for the school newspaper and director of the Qidian Drama Troupe, and successfully directed four drama plays. After graduation, she worked as an intern at *People's Daily*, *Dentsu*, *Shopee* and several other companies, engaging in advertising and public relations. She loves food, travel, photography and novels. She now lives with her parents in her hometown in China.

Index

Abbott, Matthew 130
Abe, Naoko 215
Albury, Kath 12
Alexander, Tristram 200
Allen, Paul 130
Altmann, Eduardo G. 200
Anson, Fleur 138
Arts Digital 22, 67
Arts Informatics 46–49, 113–114, 237
Austin, Robin 138
Avieson, Bunty 33, 39, 78, 79–83, 89–90, 111, 164–167, 171, 181, 210, 214, 219

Bachelor of Arts Informatics *see* Arts Informatics
Bachelor of Arts (Media and Communications) 1, 15–18, 36, 50, 52, 98, 131, 173, 177
Bachelor of Arts/Bachelor of Advanced Studies (Digital Cultures) 42
Bachelor of Arts/Bachelor of Advanced Studies (Media and Communications) 42, 52, 162
Bachelor of Arts/Bachelor of Laws (Major in Media Studies) 42, 95
Bacud, Anna Jenica 167–168, 171
Baker, Su 6
Barbagallo, Maria 67, 69, 71–73, 75
Baylosis, Cherry 193
Becherwaise, Neil 6
Bednarek, Monika 200
Behayi, Kayla 158
Blaskovic, Sonia 138
Blue, Indigo 163
Boichak, Olga 43, 53, 118–122, 200–201, 215–216
Boland-Rudder, Hamish 173–177, 181
Bollmer, Grant 28
Booth, Julia 130
Borschke, Margie 43
Brce, Mario 68–69, 71, 75
Brennan, Joe 192

Brennan MacCallum Building 60, 64–65, 67
Brennan, Marc 11, 22, 24–25, 95
Brevini, Benedetta 28, 39, 42, 84, 186–192, 213
Broinowski, Richard 163, 173–177, 178, 209
Brown, Sharon 138
Butler, Joanne 137

Carey, Benjamin 197–199
Carter, Marcus 53, 73, 114–116, 119–122, 193
Cass, Bettina 1
Castillo, Antonio 20, 25
Castino, Lauren 170, 171
Caulfield, Matt 138
Centre for Digital Technologies and Societies 53, 121
Chaidaroon, Sean 20, 126
Chapman, Simon 151
Charley, Peter 107–108
Chesher, Chris xvi, 47, 48, 113–114, 116, 120–121, 136, 215
Chester, Diana 197–199
Chrysanthos, Natassia 164
Cleland, Kathy xvi, 47–48, 51, 113
collaborations
  domestic 37, 153, 195–205
  industry 25, 31, 40, 84, 129, 141, 144, 164–171
  international 20, 22, 26, 33–34, 121–122, 173–181, 203, 207–219
Computational Social Sciences Lab 53
Connor, Elizabeth 98
Cooney, Sam 137
Corbett, David 138

Couch, Rowanne 137
Cousins, Lucy 137
COVID-19 xx, 40–41, 57, 66, 73–75, 121, 142, 147–149, 152, 154, 158, 168–169, 181, 190, 193, 197, 208, 221–232, 238–240
Coyte, Matt 137
Craig, Jacob 67, 70, 75
Crawford, Kate 10, 20, 28, 95, 204
Crowe, Christine 48

Davies, Clare 132, 158
Deitz, Milissa 12
Dena, Christy 192
Deshpande, Vaibhavi 116
Digital Cultures xvi, 28, 37, 45–55, 60, 63, 113–123, 188, 192, 235, 237, 241–242
Digital Cultures Research Cluster 53, 121
Digital Media Unit 22, 60–64, 67–76, 145, 228
digitalisation xvi, 4, 10, 16, 28, 31, 37–38, 43, 45, 49–52, 54, 68, 85, 96–97, 109–111, 114, 122–123, 132, 135–136, 140, 202–204, 209, 211, 215, 236–237, 241–243; *see also* social media
Donald, Stephanie Hemelryk 211
Dowton, Josh 68
Dunn, Anne 7–8, 11–12, 16–21, 24–28, 59, 94–95, 102–103, 185–186
Duvall, Andrea 137
Dwyer, Timothy 20, 27, 58, 61, 63, 103, 108–109, 204, 211–212

Index

Education Building 59, 63–65, 71, 228
Egliston, Ben 43, 53, 193
Evans, Geraint 7, 95

Faculty of Arts and Social Sciences 1–2, 5–6, 9, 14, 15, 21, 23, 40, 43, 58, 63, 66, 67, 69, 73, 101, 113, 137, 191, 223, 225, 236
Fay, David 67
Fekete, Alan 46
Feng, Lydia 177–179, 181
Fernandez, Rochelle 137
Fernando, Marc 68, 74, 145
Fiford, Deonie 137
Fitzpatrick, Tim 22
Flew, Terry 41, 43, 53, 54, 66, 123, 211, 218, 235–237, 242
Flynn, Justin 67
Foley, Bernadette 141
Fray, Peter 24
Funnell, Linda 141

Garton, Stephen 5
Giles, Fiona 20, 21, 23, 24, 26, 42, 84, 95, 108, 135–138, 142, 144, 147–149, 151, 210, 218
Glen, Philip 22, 61–62, 64, 67–72, 76, 145
Goggin, Gerard 20, 24, 25, 38, 40, 41, 43, 73, 188, 193, 204–205, 207–209, 211, 215, 217–219
Gray, Joanne 43, 53
Griffith, Mikaela 179–181

Habib, Jawahir 158
Hage, Ghassan 12
Hartley, John 43
Hernandez, Adriana 164–169, 175
Hespanhol, Luke 198

Higher Degree Research program 39, 43, 53, 183–193
master's by research 189
PhD xviii, 10, 12, 84, 122, 132, 183–193
Hobbs, Mitchell 125–133, 202–203, 205
Holme Building 51, 57–61, 64, 72
honours 13, 42, 95, 162, 186, 189
Hub for Innovation in Podcasting 37
Humphries, Gary 138
Humphry, Justine 35, 48–49, 53, 117–121, 201–202, 215
Hutchinson, Jonathon 28, 29, 39–40, 96, 104, 186, 190, 201, 211, 215, 218

Innis, Michelle 130
internationalisation 11, 31, 33–36, 65, 85, 102–105, 207–219, 242; see also Overseas Fellowship Program, collaborations: international, students: international
internship 2, 13, 20, 33, 84, 95, 106, 108, 143, 149, 161–171; see also Overseas Fellowship Program
Ivers, Roberta 137
Ivison, Duncan 12

Jagose, Annamarie 50, 60, 98
Jeffery, Catherine Page 43, 130
John Woolley Building 32, 51, 58, 60–63, 65, 70, 90
Johnson, Mark 53, 118–123
Jonson, Annemarie 46
Josephi, Beate 218–219

Katz, Louise 23
Kim, Ho-Seong 209
Koziol, Michael 164

Lambrinos, Stephen 67
Landa, Miriam 113, 116–117, 123
Lane, Daragh 67
Langker, Adrian 67
Launder, Charlotte 131
Le Masurier, Megan 20, 23, 83–84, 109, 137–143, 147–148, 183–184
Ledbury, Mark 37
LeMay, Amanda 138
Lewis, Nicole 115–117, 123
Linsdell, Claire 137
Lucine, Blue 68, 71
Lumby, Catharine 1–2, 3, 6–14, 16–20, 23–25, 28, 41, 57, 84, 93–95, 98–99, 131, 162–163, 183–186

Maguire, Anna 137, 140–141
Mahoney, Tyler 70
Mann, Alana 20, 27, 31–32, 35, 42, 126, 163–164, 195–197, 210
Manner, Richard 68–69
Mao, Lynette (Yue) 224–225, 227–228
Maras, Steven 12–13, 20–25, 26, 35, 42, 67, 84, 95, 185–186, 209, 218
Markson, Sharri 91–93, 96, 99
Martin, Fiona 20, 25, 28, 33, 37–40, 43, 49–50, 57–59, 62–66, 73, 84, 86, 95–98, 105, 163, 175, 204, 211, 218–219, 223–227, 231

Master of Digital Communication and Culture 42, 46, 48, 51, 113–123, 136, 237
Master of Health Communication 19–20, 25, 42, 132, 151–159
Master of Media Practice 13, 18–20, 36, 42, 101–112, 148, 167–168, 209, 224
Master of Publishing 19, 42, 83–84, 135–150
Master of Strategic Public Relations 19, 42, 125–133
Matalov, Tina 109
Maxwell, Ian 217
Mayer, Henry 4
McCarthy, Michael 67
McDiarmid, Rachael 141
McDonald, Barbara 6
McHardy, Franscois 137
McHugh, Siobhán 37
McKinnon, Alex 92
McNamara, Kim 183–184
Media@Sydney 189, 217
Metzl, Sharon 138
Modjeska, Drusilla 144
Moffat, Robin 163–164, 169, 175, 209
Morrison, Rodney 141
Mrva-Montoya, Agata 43, 138–142, 145, 148
Munro, Craig 137
Munro, Jay 158

Nguyen, Jessie 130
Nip, Joyce 20, 32, 105, 186, 188–189, 212

O'Byrne, Cheryl 116

Index

O'Donnell, Penny xix, 20, 25, 35–36, 40, 85, 87, 91–93, 96, 103, 186–188, 204, 210
O'Flynn, Olivia 109
Old Teachers' College 63
Ong, Victoria 106, 108
Ormeno, Julieta 138
O'Shea, Nicola 137
Overseas Fellowship Program 85, 163, 173–181

pandemic *see* COVID-19
Parallax 85, 177, 180
Pattison, Pip 98
Pefanis, Julian 46
Perna, Tony 116
Pesce, Mark 37
Piccione, Tim 168–169
Porter, Michaella 158

Ray, Alison 79, 82–83, 88–89, 105
RC Mills Building 57–58, 59
Redfern, Lea 37, 79–83, 87, 89, 109–111, 141, 229–231
Reinhold, Leigh 137
Reng, Xiang 43
Riegel, Jeff 211
Ross, Andrew 200
Rossiter, Mark 145

Sainty, Lane 92
Salience 85
Santangelo, Dominic 57, 59
Schlosberg, David 203
School of Art, Communication and English 42, 98, 242
School of English, Art History, Film and Media 46

School of Literature, Art and Media 50, 60, 67, 69, 74, 98, 188, 211, 242
Shen, Gang 106, 108
Singhal, Pallavi 164
social media xvi, 28, 38, 49, 52, 65, 89, 92, 96–97, 104, 108–109, 111, 115, 128, 140, 154, 166, 183, 200–202, 211, 237
Social Sciences Building 70
Socio-Technical Futures Lab 121, 193
Sorrenson, Katherine 138
Spence, Alexandra 68
Spence, Michael 221
Stanton, Richard 11, 95, 126
Stanton, Shelagh 68, 71–72, 75
Stepnik, Agata 190
Stevenson, Keith 145
Stoll, Nick 92
Stronach, Gregor 137, 145
Student Anthology xx, 144–149
students
  diversity xvii, 4, 18, 158
  international xvii, 19, 33–36, 41, 66, 101, 103, 105, 109, 114, 189, 207, 219, 222–228, 231–232, 236–238, 240
  numbers 5, 20, 31–33, 40, 42, 49, 53, 65, 68, 101, 109–111, 113, 148, 181, 189, 222, 230, 232, 236
Su, Meizi 43
Sutherland, Chelsea 146
Swiatek, Lukasz 192
Sydney College of the Arts 5, 63, 69–70, 75, 108, 138, 242
Sydney Games & Play Lab 53

Tattersall, Amanda 37

Technology and Culture Reading
    Group 28
Teh, David 47
Thurtell, Louise 137
Tiffen, Rod 6
Tindall, Sally 130
Tonkin, John 47–48, 113
Transient Building 58, 60, 64
Truong, Mabel 202

Van Heekeren, Margaret 34, 85, 88,
    98, 221–223, 230, 232
Vette, Kaitlyn 158
Vromen, Ariadne 38

Wadiwel, Dinesh 204
Walker, Pam 77–79, 83, 89–90

Walsh, Richard 137
Wang, Hanlin 117
Ward, Michael 190
Waterhouse, Anna 198
Watson, Lucy 192
Weatherall, Kim 38
Werder, Olaf 25, 132, 151–153,
    157–158, 199–200, 213
Wickham, Shelley 198
Work-Integrated Learning 40
Wrigley, Jodie 158
Wu, Yulan 117

Yang, Lan 116–117

www.ingramcontent.com/pod-product-compliance
Lightning Source LLC
Chambersburg PA
CBHW042129160426
43198CB00022B/2952